SMART LEARNING

A Study Skills Guide for Teens

SMART LEARNING

A Study Skills Guide for Teens

William Christen and Thomas Murphy

Edited by Deborah B. and William C. Strother

Cover Art by Addie Seabarkrob
Book Design by Victoria Voelker

Library of Congress Cataloging-in-Publication Data

Christen, William L.
   Smart learning: a study skills guide for teens/William Christen
and Thomas Murphy.
   p. cm.
   Includes index.
   Summary: Suggests strategies for effective study, including note
taking, writing, time management, goal setting, and organization
in general.
   ISBN 0-9628556-5-0
   1. Study, Method of--Handbooks, manuals, etc.--Juvenile literature. [1. Study, Method of.]   I. Murphy, Thomas, 1949 Mar. 9 -
II. Title.
LB1049.C54384   373.13'02812--dc20   91-48274

Grayson Bernard Publishers
233 S. Pete Ellis Drive, Suite 12
P.O. Box 5247
Bloomington, Indiana 47407

About the Authors

Thomas Murphy currently is teaching eighth-grade Language Arts at Sunrise Middle School in Phoenix, Arizona. Tom has been a classroom teacher and a principal for nineteen years. He holds a B.A. in Elementary Education and an M.A. in School Administration. Tom is co-author of a student management system entitled *The Skillful Learner*. He has had numerous workshops for teachers, parents, and students throughout the country.

Dr. William Christen is currently working as the Director of Social Studies/Science in an inner-city school district in Phoenix, Arizona. He has been a middle school teacher, college administrator, professor, principal, and consultant for the past twenty-three years. Bill is the senior author of a series of study skills books for elementary, middle school and high school students published in 1984. His motto, "work smarter, not harder" is the heart of the philosophy of this book. He is co-author of *The Skillful Learner* student organizer presently available.

Contents

Changes
Help from a Friend
The Finale

Now for the Coming Attractions: Previewing
The Title of the Show
Skip the Introductions? Definitely Not!
Using Your Head(ings)
Just Picture This
Questions First

Let's Get Hyper: Reading and Studying Actively
A Real Reading Workout: Read Flexibly
The Hunt Is On: Find the Topic, Main Ideas, and
Details
The Supporting Cast: Learn to Separate Topic, Main
Ideas, and Details
Getting It Down: Take Notes for Later Study

Elementary, My Dear Watson: Examining
When to Ask *When*, And Other Questions
How Do You Get Started Asking Questions?
Now You've Got the (Main) Idea

Heating Up Cold Storage: Prompting
Reaching Into the Freezer
The Big Bonus
Togetherness — It Pays Off

Me, Myself, and i
Mapping Your Thoughts
Splitting the Page: SSS (Split Summary System)
Making It Work

Beating the Time Crunch
Lists, Lists, Lists
What It'll Take

Introduction

Learning belongs to you. Like your beagle pup or the soccer ball you got for Christmas, it's yours.

But unlike the puppy or the ball, learning has been with you from the instant you were born, and it will be with you even after you grow up — even after you are older than your grandparents.

You can do a lot with learning — or you can choose to do very little. We hope you do a lot.

Learning is magic. It can open up the whole world for you. It can show you why clocks tick, how Eskimos live, where gold was discovered. It can point to the farthest star. It can tell you where the deepest mysteries of the universe remain.

You learn all your life. What's important is what and how much you choose to learn and how well you do it. Smart learning, the kind we talk about in this book, will help you learn more — faster, better, and easier than you did before.

This book is your tool box. The tools in it can make you a really good student. In fact, we think your grades should go up one letter grade if you just read the book and use the tools every day.

But there are no shortcuts.

You have to read the book carefully and follow our instructions closely to make the most of what's in the box.

If you decided to build a dog house, just having the right tools wouldn't make it a good dog house. You would have to know how to use those tools and how to follow the building directions. Then you could make that pup of yours the perfect home.

It's the same with learning. You need to become an expert at using the tools we describe in this book so that you can become a smart learner — for the rest of your life.

Chapter One tells you about the ingredients of smart learning. It includes some important tips and answers some questions that most kids ask about learning. There's even a chart to help you find the best place to study and a questionnaire to find out what kind of learner you are now. You can use the questionnaire again when you finish the book to see how much you've improved.

Chapter Two tells you how to be an active learner, and offers better ways to read, listen, and write.

Chapter Three has important information about writing, including how to write reports, something you will do a lot of in high school and college.

Chapter Four teaches you a foolproof study system that has four parts: previewing, reading and studying actively, examining, and prompting.

Chapter Five explains three different ways to take notes and shows examples of each.

In the rest of the book you'll learn how best to use the tools in the chapters above. Chapter Six will teach you better ways to manage your time. Chapter Seven shows you how to prepare for and take tests. And in Chapter Eight, you'll learn how to set goals, big and little, short-term and long-term.

1

What It Takes

Burning to Learn

All kids — and that includes you — can become smart learners. But you won't get there by wishing. Instead, you must follow three important steps:

- Use a variety of learning tools.
- Allow enough time to learn.
- Find ways to get help when you need it.

But before you can take the first step you need to develop three keys to success — effort, curiosity, and a strong desire to learn.

Effort is essential to smart learning, or active learning as we call it in this book, the kind of learning you do when you attack work instead of just doing enough to get by. Passive learners are not smart learners. They're not learners at all, really. They're the kids who let things happen to them — usually bad things, such as getting D's. And they groan when they get them.

Curiosity is essential to active learning. Being curious means asking questions and not being discouraged when the answers aren't right the first time. Make learning a treasure hunt in which the hunt itself, not just finding the treasure, is the fun part. Curious learners look at a problem from a lot of different directions, and work out connections between pieces of the puzzle.

Like a lot of things that are really worthwhile, active learning requires hard work, concentration, and time. Learn to believe in hard work and give yourself enough time to do it. Make up your mind that you *want* to learn. Set some goals and figure out a way to reward yourself when you reach them. Smart learning is impossible unless you really want to learn. Say to yourself "I want to become a better student." Find someone to imitate who has a strong desire to learn. Talk with that person about his or her study habits and imitate them.

Be enthusiastic. Enthusiasm is contagious. It carries over to those around you, including your teachers, who say enthusiastic learners are the most fun to teach. Enthusiasm and positive mental attitudes generate energy and energy can become effort.

Now that you have made up your mind that you want to learn, that you will let your curiosity go wild and that you will give learning your best effort, it's time to move on to some important questions that kids like you have asked about smart learning.

A Few Questions

How can I improve my concentration on school work? Learning to concentrate requires some planning plus effort, enthusiasm, and desire to learn, of course. The following tips will help you focus your energy so you can concentrate.

• *Set a learning goal.* Write down the exact assignment. Make sure you know what you need to do, how much time you will need to complete the work, and that you have the necessary tools and materials to begin the task.

• *Choose a quiet place to study.* Noise of any kind, including music, will distract you. The evidence on this point is irrefutable from study after study! Studying in front of the TV or listening to music will not help you concentrate.

- *Set a study time.* Carve out two regular study times for each day. This routine will allow you to get more done in less time because you will be better organized and less tired.
- *Make time for breaks.* Give each task a time limit. We suggest you work in half-hour segments. Then take five to ten minutes off. Stretch, have a piece of fruit, get something to drink. Then go on to the next task. Researchers have found that the average adult can only concentrate on new information for 20 minutes at a time. You will need the extra 10 minutes of each half-hour segment to plan what comes next.
- *Get actively involved.* If you want to concentrate on your work, you need to get involved with it. Ask yourself questions. Take notes. Plan a strategy. Learn new words by taking the time to look them up. Discuss the material with a study pal.

Is my space the best place? Finding a quiet study place at home is essential. Use the Interruption Chart below to find some area in your home that will be a quiet place for studying.

Interruption Chart

To find a good study place, fill out the chart below. For each of the places you list, put a check mark in the correct column if the statement is true for that place. The column with the least checks is the best place to study.

	Place 1	Place 2	Place 3
1. Everybody, even the dog, interrupts me when I study here.	___	___	___
2. I take too many breaks when I study here.	___	___	___
3. TV sitcoms, my brother's stereo, or rockin' radio blare too loudly when I study here.	___	___	___
4. My breaks are too long when I study here.	___	___	___
5. I talk too much when I study here.	___	___	___
6. I'm on the phone too much when I should be studying here.	___	___	___
7. It's too hot or too cold here to study without frying or freezing.	___	___	___
8. Chair, table, and lighting arrangements here don't help.	___	___	___
9. When I study here, I am often distracted by certain people, such as noisy little brothers or sisters.	___	___	___
Total checks	___	___	___

The best place for me to study is

_____

What's the inventory? Take a few minutes to see how well you are doing right now. Many kids think they have good study habits, yet they don't finish assignments on time or they don't get started on them when they should. They doodle and dawdle. Doodling is OK, but much dawdling isn't. Take a few minutes and complete the following study skills questionnaire. Take it again after you've finished the book and practiced using the skills.

Study Skills Questionnaire

Circle the appropriate number for each of the following statements that applies to you. Don't worry if you don't understand words like mapping and the ῖ format — we'll explain them later. If you already know them, well, you're a step ahead.

A = Always; M = Most of the time; S = Sometimes;
R = Rarely; N = Never

	A	M	S	R	N

Study System

1. I preview assignments before I read them.   1 2 3 4 5
2. I read with a pencil in my hand.   1 2 3 4 5
3. I study by asking myself the kind of questions my teacher might ask.   1 2 3 4 5
4. I recite answers when preparing for examination questions.   1 2 3 4 5
5. I predict what information will come next.   1 2 3 4 5

Taking Notes and Organization

6. My class notes are organized by three levels (topic, main ideas, and details).   1 2 3 4 5
7. I take notes as I read my assignments.   1 2 3 4 5
8. I use mapping strategies to organize information.   1 2 3 4 5
9. I use the Ⅱ format for taking notes.   1 2 3 4 5
10. I use the SSS format for taking notes.   1 2 3 4 5
11. My notebook is easy to understand.   1 2 3 4 5
12. I listen, then write my notes during class.   1 2 3 4 5

Time Management

13. I make a daily schedule and stick to it.   1 2 3 4 5
14. I use a monthly calendar to manage long-term assignments   1 2 3 4 5
15. I start my assignments with a purpose and a goal in mind.   1 2 3 4 5
16. I do a task analysis on complicated long-term assignments.   1 2 3 4 5

Homework

17. I get my homework assignments done on time.   1 2 3 4 5
18. I quickly make up assignments after absences.   1 2 3 4 5
19. I have a quiet place where I can do my homework.   1 2 3 4 5
20. I put studying before outside activities.   1 2 3 4 5

Test Taking

21. On essay tests I plan before I write.   1 2 3 4 5
22. I manage my time well during tests.   1 2 3 4 5
23. I study for tests in small parts rather than cramming all at once.   1 2 3 4 5
24. I read directions twice before I begin to answer the questions.   1 2 3 4 5
25. I preview tests to see the type and point values of each question.   1 2 3 4 5

Habits and Attitudes
26. I get enough rest to feel physically ready to go to class. 1 2 3 4 5
27. I am able to study without daydreaming. 1 2 3 4 5
28. I go to class prepared. 1 2 3 4 5
29. I am proud of myself as a learner. 1 2 3 4 5

Writing Reports
30. I follow the writing process when preparing an essay or term paper. 1 2 3 4 5
31. I use proofreader's symbols when editing. 1 2 3 4 5
32. I use a writing guide checklist to help me manage my writing. 1 2 3 4 5
33. I use mapping as a way to preorganize a writing assignment. 1 2 3 4 5
34. I use a writing calendar to help me keep track of my project. 1 2 3 4 5

Now that you have completed the questionnaire, take some time to analyze the results. For each of the sections of the questionnaire, see how you have done.

Study System	How many Rarelys or Nevers did you mark? If you have half or more marked as Rarely or Never, you need to pay special attention to Chapter Four.
Taking Notes and Organization	If you have half or more statements marked as Rarely or Never, Chapter Five will help you.
Time Management	If you have half or more statements marked Rarely or Never, refer to Chapters Six and Eight.
Test Taking	If you have half or more statements marked as Rarely or Never, see Chapter Seven.
Habits and Attitudes	If you have half or more statements marked as Rarely or Never in these two areas, pay attention to Chapters One and Two.
Writing Reports	If you have half or more statements marked as Rarely or Never, see Chapter Three.

How can my textbooks help me? Most people think a textbook is something they can read cover to cover, like a novel. But textbooks aren't novels. Often they are not that interesting or even well written. They aren't intended to be literature. In fact, you will get the most out of your textbooks if you do *not* read them like novels. Textbooks contain facts for you to use, and it's OK to take only what you need. You don't have to read the entire book, one page after another. Instead, learn to use the special help the author provides — the index, chapter summaries, whatever's there — to get to what you really need. You can save yourself lots of time if you figure out how your book works early in the school year. Use the chart below to discover the aids the author has included in each textbook you are now using in school.

Getting to Know My Textbook

Make a copy or photocopy of the following chart for each of your textbooks, or using the chart below, write a separate list of the aids that each of your textbooks contains.

My textbook has the following aids
____ Preface or introduction

____ Table of contents

____ Glossary

____ Subject index

____ Author index

____ Charts, graphs, diagrams

____ Italics, boldface for emphasis

____ Questions at end of chapter

____ Margin notes

____ Footnotes

____ Pronunciation helps for new terms

____ Chapter introduction

____ Chapter pre-reading questions

____ Chapter summaries

How are new vocabulary words introduced?
____ bold type

____ italics

____ footnotes

____ margin notes

____ colored ink

____ defined in text

____ vocabulary list at beginning of Chapter

____ vocabulary list at end of Chapter

____ vocabulary list at beginning of each section in Chapter

What is the copyright date of the textbook?

Skim each chapter in the table of contents. Make a list on a separate sheet of paper of any new term that you do not understand. Make your list chapter-by-chapter.

The Smart Learning Tool Box

Now that you understand about active learning, effort, enthusiasm, and desire to learn, it's time to tell you about some of the tools you will be using.

The first tools we offer can be your Ten Commandments of Learning. They are common sense really, but it's surprising how many kids forget them. Read them carefully and try to memorize them. They are the basic rules of learning.

1. Set up a routine. Save time for homework in the morning and evening. Pace yourself. Set a limit on the time you will spend working. Use a timer or set your wrist watch. When the buzzer sounds, stop and take a break. When you lose energy, you lose the winner's edge. Have a fruit snack to avoid the problem. Some people even eat smaller meals at regular intervals five to seven times a day. It's also a good idea to go to bed at the same time each day and to watch your eating habits!

After your break, you will have more energy and will be better able to concentrate.

2. Be prepared. The first two weeks of every school year or semester are very important, so come to the classroom well prepared. Make sure you have the right equipment. Begin with a three-ring binder with dividers, two erasable pens, two mechanical pencils, a hi-lighter felt marker for marking important text, a small stapler, a small stick-on pad, and a six-inch ruler. That's a basic supply kit that can vary as teachers and courses require.

3. Pay attention, especially as class begins and ends. Teachers often use the first and last five minutes of the period to go over the main points of the lesson. At the end of class, you may get an announcement of a quiz, or hear about homework or tests. Write assignments and due dates in the assignment section of your notebook or three-ring binder.

4. Turn in homework. The single biggest reason kids get D's and F's is because they don't turn in class work and homework assignments. Enough said.

5. Focus on your work, not your friends. Find a corner of the classroom where you won't be tempted to talk. Focus your attention on the teacher and your notes.

6. Find a study pal. Make one friend a study pal, someone you can share phone time with to check your progress or go over tough problems.

7. Work ahead. Read ahead of the teacher. Try to stay about ten pages in front of the class. You'll have a better idea about the subject, and you'll be able to see where the day's lesson fits into where you've been and where you're going. You will also know what information is not included in the textbook but given to you by your teacher.

8. Analyze your textbooks. Early in the school year figure out how your textbook is organized. The person who wrote it is trying to help you learn by giving you study ideas. Learn the key terms. Go over the chapter reviews and chapter questions. Look at the index, check for a glossary and other study helps.

9. Ask questions. Listen to the questions your teacher asks. Most of the questions will be one of the five W's: Who? What? When? Where? Why? These are the questions you must learn to ask yourself and the teacher when you don't understand something.

10. Organize your notebook. Make a separate section of your notebook for each of your classes. A three-ring binder allows you to add, subtract, or more importantly, rearrange pages. Think of your notebook as you might a stamp collection. It is never completed. You will always collect more and more pages to make it more valuable. Your notebook is the first source of the important information you will need to know about a subject. You will have to read and reread what goes into your notebook.

Think ahead. What key sections do you need for each class? Does the class have a language of its own, like science or math? If so, you may want to create your own personal glossary of terms. Is there a lot of opinion writing, as in literature? Keep a journal section where you can work out your opinions. Does the class require you to work out problems? Create a daily work section. It's impossible to overemphasize the importance of the notebook in the learning process.

A notebook is like a camera. It allows you to freeze time. While it doesn't record pictures of events, it keeps your good ideas (and the teacher's) from evaporating in the same way a camera preserves a moment. The trick is to find an effective note taking system that doesn't take too much time so that you can keep all those good ideas, not just a few of them.

Keep a separate section of your notebook for long-term assignments. Set dates for starting and finishing the work, and then break it into small chunks. Pace yourself. Do a little each day. Most students wait until a few days before the assignment is due. Then they freak out and stay up until midnight or later to try and finish. Procrastinators often do poorly because they did not give themselves enough time to work on any but the easiest parts of the assignment.

That's the basic 10. There's one more, of course, but that's the most obvious.

Go to school every day. A+ students hardly ever miss school. If you do have to miss school because of an illness or accident, find out what lessons you missed and turn in make-up assignments as quickly as possible.

These 10 commandments are your most basic tools. They're the saw and hammer in your tool box of smart learning tools. How well you learn to use them will determine your success . . . or failure to learn smart.

Learn to use them well. Overprepare for your classes, and let the first grades in the teacher's grade book be A's. The first two weeks are crucial. So begin the A habit early — you'll like how it feels.

Remember . . .

Using the 10 commandments of smart learning can mean immediate pay-offs for you. Taking control of your schoolwork and getting things done on time are two goals you must achieve. The desire to learn and to become an A student are worthy goals. Creating effective work and study habits will help you to learn the value of hard work and also to enjoy the benefits.

2

Active Learning

Now that you've learned — and are practicing — the ten commandments of smart learning, you're beginning to see what it feels like to be a good student. Your grades are rising faster than the thermometer on a hot summer day, right? Well, maybe not that fast, but they're looking better.

It's now time to rev up and be an *active* learner. Lots of kids think all they need to do to get by is to be polite guests in class, but you already know that simply taking up space won't help you achieve your goals. This is especially true when you are in middle school and later in high school. To succeed in secondary school you must be an active learner who knows how to:

- learn from reading
- be flexible in your thinking, adapting what you already know to new information and ideas — be able to give up on bad ideas
- check your own progress rather than always relying on someone else (usually your teacher) for the OK to continue
- recognize the things you don't know
- get help from a lot of places, and continue to look for that help until you find it (It's sort of like when you played hide-and-seek as a little kid — you wouldn't have given up then just because you didn't find anyone the first place you looked.)

- make it your job, not somebody else's, to learn assignments.

Pumping Up: The Process

Just what goes on when learning happens? Can the teacher just pour the information into your brain like in the cartoons? Or can you simply memorize it all? Well, classrooms aren't filling stations, and your brain can't just get topped up with useful bits and pieces of information. And while memory is important in learning, it's only one part of five stages to active learning.

The process of active learning — smart learning — includes the following stages:

• Gathering information	looking it up or finding it out
• Recording information	writing it down in a disciplined and orderly way
• Organizing and making sense of information	making good notes; putting information into long-term memory
• Retrieving information	being able to find and decipher your notes
• Using information	making all of the above work for you so that you understand what it's all about — writing an A paper or acing a test

Gathering information. The first thing you need to do is collect information that's already known about the topic. And there's an awful lot of information already out there about practically everything. You can find information in textbooks, from movies shown in class, from lessons, from magazines, and museums. Sometimes, the most important source turns out to be other people. A classroom of middle school students once learned a whole lot about their own town's history when they interviewed retired coal miners and miners' wives about the coalfields that had been active in their area decades earlier.

Recording information. Facts from the encyclopedia on Japanese geography or from the interviews of retired miners would be lost without some means of recording them. Gathering information is a lot like holding an icicle. You know you've got it while it's there, but when it melts away, it's gone. Your notebook is your deep freeze — your record. If it's new information, write it down. But be sure you don't clutter up your notebook with too much trivial stuff. The way you make notes is important — so important that we're going to show you three ways of doing it in Chapter Five. You'll be able to use any or all of the three throughout the school year.

Organizing and making sense of information.

You've come a long way, now. You've gathered the information and you've got it safely tucked away in your notes. So all that's left is memorizing it, right?

Wrong. Just memorizing it won't mean you understand it. $E = MC^2$ is easy to memorize, but just memorizing Einstein's formula for the theory of relativity is an awfully long way from really understanding what it means. It would take years of study in math and physics to get close to that.

In a more everyday way, you must do the same with real learning of any sort. Understanding comes from fitting the many small chunks of information you've gathered into a pattern that shows the overall picture. You see how things relate to one another. You can even develop new patterns with what you know. You organize the material in order to understand it.

Retrieving information. Your brain can hold as many as ten million volumes of information. That's a lot of books. The trick is how to pull out the bits you need when you need them, the same as with the card catalogue in the library (whether it's computerized or still on index cards). We'll help you with that in Chapter Five, when we explain mapping, a note-taking system that groups information into clusters for easier retrieval from your own memory.

Using information. The report, the speech, the solution to the problem are the finished products of your sharpened communications skills. This is where you show that you really do know something about Japanese geography, or about how coal miners lived at the turn of the century — or even, if you work at it long enough, about Einstein's theory. You are applying what you have learned.

If you know how to add and subtract in school, but get cheated every time somebody makes change for you, you haven't really learned addition or subtraction very well.

In school, if you can't compare, create, compose, classify, produce, devise, categorize, prove, illustrate, or group the information you've learned, you haven't really learned it very well.

If you've really learned well, you'll be able to graph, diagram, produce an article, make a report, write a story, solve the problem, do a survey — whatever it is that demonstrates you've learned well.

The Skills

There are four essential communications skills: reading, listening, speaking, and writing. But you can't simply read, listen, talk, and write. To make the most of these tools you must *actively* read, listen, talk, and write.

Active reading. Most readers just read. Books are either easy and interesting to most readers or so hard student readers don't even try to understand them without help from their parents or teachers.

Active readers are different. They ask, "What do I already know about this topic?" And they don't just ask themselves the question, they write down what they know.

Ask questions of the material you're reading and take notes as you go along. That's active reading.

Use the textbook check sheet on page 7 to figure out what helpful aids the author has provided. Use those aids in decoding the message in all those words. That's active reading.

If you just let your eyes go over the words without doing something to make sense of them, you're wasting a lot of your valuable time. You may be working hard, but you're not working smart!

Active reading is likely to be different from what you're used to doing in school. Much of school reading is *passive* reading. Up till now, you may have been taught to answer questions like those found in the teacher's manual, and to go no further.

You were taught to answer questions, not to ask them. The questions you answered would show how much you knew about the details of the story, but not necessarily what the story meant. And you may have been taught only to answer the questions that agreed with the author's opinion, but not to test your own thinking.

As a result, you were taught that the teacher's manual is the place to go for the right answers, and you shouldn't depend on yourself too much. You've learned that textbooks are always right, that the printed word is always right, and that you really shouldn't question the facts as they appear in the book — not ever.

Active reading will allow you to question such ideas. Thinking and learning are social activities. You need to discuss your ideas and those of the author with others — your teacher and classmates for a start. You need to talk and argue, and you'll get better the more you do. You'll also learn to listen better and pull out and keep the best bits of what others say. You'll learn to use the evidence from your reading to prove the soundness of your ideas.

Active reading is slow reading, with pencil in hand. It's not the same as reading books just for fun. Always stop and ask yourself what the author means.

As you read, reach to the new material. Ask yourself how you feel about this information. What are the new ideas the author is presenting? Make notes of your responses. It is hard to keep responses in your head, and you don't want to lose your first reactions. They might evaporate forever if you don't write them down. You can later use your notes to connect new ideas to old ones.

Active readers:
- *preview the material **before** reading.*
- *read with a pencil in their hands.*
- *always begin with a purpose for reading in mind.*
- *record new terms or key words.* If you can't figure out the meaning from the context, look up the term in a dictionary or glossary.
- *note important passages.* Make a note of the page number and paragraph so you can return to that part for further study.
- *form opinions.* Ask yourself how you feel about the author's words and whether you agree or disagree with his or her views.
- *read additional material.* Do other books or articles present opinions that are different from the author's?
- *talk with others about the material.*
- *ask questions.* What did I know about this topic before reading the assignment? What is the author really trying to say?
- *figure out connections.* Are there relationships among paragraphs, ideas, or characters? If you see possible connections, note them.
- *identify and understand information on different levels.* (topic, main ideas, and details).
- *decide what is important.* Learn to distinguish between important and trivial information.
- *reread.* Make sure you really know the material by rereading it; read it more than once if you are still unclear.

Listen up now. Like active readers, active listeners get involved with information they hear even before they hear it. Active listeners ask themselves what they already know about the topic and jot down questions they would like answered. They listen with a pencil in hand and take notes of the speaker's main ideas. They freeze information so they can refer to it later.

Taking notes while listening requires a great deal of concentration. Don't try to write down everything the speaker is saying. Listen for key words or terms the speaker emphasizes or repeats. Write what you hear in your own words; your notes will make more sense to you later. Take advantage of visual aids the speaker provides, such as notes on a chalkboard or overhead transparencies, and record them.

Active listening doesn't end when the speaker does. Once the presentation is over, go back and check your notes for understanding. Ask the speaker any questions you might have. Later, organize your notes. Chapter Five will tell you how to do this in more detail.

Compare your notes and thoughts about the presentation with your classmates. Don't hesitate to challenge the presentation or even to go to other sources to look up facts about the topic. The more you work with the information, the more likely you are to understand and remember it.

Be wary of bias. Speakers often have very strong opinions about their subject. Learn to separate opinion from fact.

Active listeners:
- *take notes.* They listen for the speaker's key words and main ideas and record them in writing.
- *tape record.* They tape lectures when the teacher talks more than half the class. Then they review the tape later.
- *organize their notes.*
- *ask questions.*
- *separate opinion from fact.*

Talking a good game. Active speakers rely on discussion as a valuable learning skill. Just planning to discuss something will make you think about its meaning before you begin talking, so you'll have a clear idea of what you want to say. Discussion also gives you the chance to hear new ideas. Most subjects have more meanings than any one person is likely to find, and talking will bring up those ideas. When disagreements occur about meaning, an exchange of opinion allows everyone to decide which argument makes the most sense.

Talking it out gives you the chance to prove your case. You can do that by reading aloud passages that support or illustrate your position. Others in the group will be able to look at an idea in a new way and may change their minds. Eliminating incorrect ideas is an essential part of solving problems.

Being able to present your argument in a group setting is a good sign you are moving toward understanding. Telling others what you know without a lot of hemming and hawing demonstrates your ability to communicate through speech.

Active speakers:
- *talk about and share ideas with others.*
- *recognize different points of view.*
- *exchange ideas in an open-minded way.*

Writing workout. Writing is one of the most important communication skills. Writing is a way of learning. Active writers process information; they pull thoughts together and organize them.

Active writers explore subjects and discover new ways of thinking about a subject. Most kids don't see the true purpose of writing. They see writing as something pretty boring that they have to do for teachers instead of something they want to do for themselves. Smart learners know that active writing is fun and very helpful. Chapter Three will give you specific writing ideas you can use in your class work and suggestions for writing longer papers.

Active writers:
- *Record their thoughts on paper.*
- *Organize their thoughts on paper.*
- *Report their ideas to others.*

Connecting the four communication skills. Your results will increase when you begin to integrate all of the communication skills. For example, if the teacher asks a question, write it, then organize possible answers before speaking. Or as you read a short story, collect information by taking notes as your read. Before asking a question write two or three versions of your question to be clear in what you want to know.

Remember . . .

Using the four communication skills will improve your ability to understand information. Becoming an active reader, listener, speaker, and writer will lead to smart learning.

3

Writing

The development of your writing skills goes hand in hand with your school success. Learning to write like a writer leads to thinking like a writer. And after all, the end result of your schooling should be clear thinking.

Journals

Have you ever had to keep a journal for a teacher? Many teachers assign journal writing because they want their students to be able to write more easily and more creatively. Journals are an excellent way to get comfortable with writing. Journals are also a great place to experiment with different kinds of writing and different topics.

Journals can also be a source of ideas to write about later. Professional writers keep journals and jot down ideas for new stories. Sometimes they may even write some ideas for opening paragraphs or a character description. They might even write down some interesting dialogue they hear while riding an elevator, which they can later use in a story.

School journals may or may not be read by a teacher. If your journal is to be read by others, it's a good idea to leave out words that might embarrass you or them.

Students often say they don't enjoy journal writing. They say they don't see a purpose in keeping a journal. Try to use them to supplement your homework and long-term projects, and to study for tests. Use them to record your impressions of the times you are growing up in; write about world events, or what the current fashions are. You can even do some sketches or write poetry. Have fun with your journal. The more you use it, the easier writing will become.

Learning Logs

Journals will help you improve your writing. Learning logs will give you a place to talk about the learning going on in your classes.

We recommend you keep notebooks for each of your classes. Your learning log for each class should be part of that notebook. Set aside a section of blank pages for it. Each day find time to make entries in your learning logs.

You can include the following items in your logs.

- *Maps you make for each topic.* We will present mapping in Chapter Five of the book. Mapping helps you organize information about a topic and opens your mind to seek new information from many sources.
- *Questions before and after you read.* Your learning log can be extremely helpful as a place for keeping questions together to bring up in class.
- *Answers to your questions.* Use your learning log to explore answers to questions or to document answers you gather as you read or listen to your teachers and classmates.
- *Thoughts from your reading and listening.* Your learning log is an excellent place to do some thinking on paper. If you don't get those thoughts down, you most likely will lose them.
- *Definitions for new words or expressions you come across in your reading and discussions with others.* You never know when you might want to use them in your own writing.

Term Papers and Reports

Getting a topic and getting started on a longer paper for a class is probably the hardest part about writing. If you have been using journals or learning logs, you already have a good start for most papers you will write for classes. But even before choosing your topic, you should make a plan that will help get the job done.

Setting a writing calendar. Before beginning a writing project such as a term paper or report, it is a good idea to make a writing calendar. Usually you will have several weeks or longer to complete a term paper or report. For example, your science teacher might assign a science report on the extinction of certain animals, or your social studies teacher might want you to write about a current social problem. In both cases you would have two to four weeks to complete the assignment. In each case, you would want to make a writing calendar for yourself.

A writing calendar is similar to the Monthly Planner we will discuss later and can be adapted from the same form. See the example on the next page. You would want to mark on the calendar the due dates for the projects, and when different parts of the job should be done. For example, your teacher might have set dates for topics to be selected and for rough drafts to be in, as well as the final due date for the project. In addition, you will want to reserve blocks of time on the calendar to finish various parts of the job. You'll set your own deadlines for the information-gathering phase and the organizational phase, and reserve writing time. You will also include time for a read-through of the rough draft by someone else, and then time to make revisions. Finally, you'll want to reserve plenty of time — at least three days — to complete the project. The plan will help you manage your time and the project so that you will not be in a mad rush at the end. In the example we've provided, the student has already chosen her topic, recycling efforts in her community.

Writing Calendar

Teacher _**Mrs. Piccolo**_____ Class _**English**_____

Project / Topic____**Recycling efforts in our community**_____

Due _____

Monthly Planner | Month |

Monday	Tuesday	Wednesday	Thursday	Friday	Weekend

Choosing a topic. Research has shown that students do a better job of writing if they select their own topics. Not all teachers will have students select their topics, because their experience is that students expect to be assigned topics. However, most teachers will allow you to use your own topic if you ask. There are also times when teachers will assign topics so students will learn more about a particular thing. Either way, go to your journal or learning log to see if there is a topic, or information about an assigned topic, you already have ideas about.

As you begin work, you also might ask what the grading criteria are for the project, provided you haven't already been told.

If you are selecting your own topic, you will probably choose something you are already interested in. Or you may choose a topic you want to know more about. If you are unfamiliar with the topic, you may not know how or where to get information. Many students in this situation go straight to the encyclopedia and begin copying or summarizing the information they find. This is a good way to get started as long as you then turn to other sources of information.

Once you have selected a topic you should approach it as you do when you read something new. Do a cluster to see what you already know. Below is an example of a cluster on wolves:

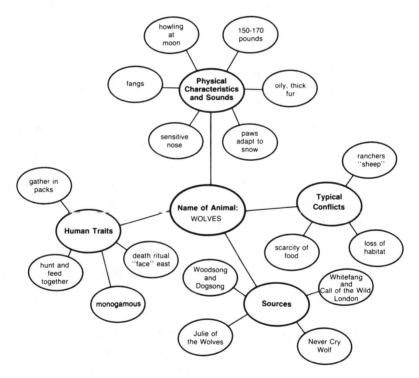

You can see that the author of this cluster knows some things about wolves, especially about how wolves are described in literature. The writer also knows there are lots of different conflicts over wolves in today's world. And he or she knows wolves have many human traits. If this were your cluster, would you add anything?

Getting the scoop. If you were going to write a paper about wolves right now, you wouldn't have a lot to go on. You have a number of decisions to make. First of all, ask yourself "What do I know about this topic?" Looking at the cluster, you have several possibilities for a paper. You could write one very long paper and discuss all the different things you know about wolves. But looking at the cluster, you can tell there are lots of separate, smaller topics from which to choose. One common mistake made in writing longer papers is making the topic too big. Focus on one aspect of a topic and do a good job of writing about that.

In this case, the author of the paper sees four topics he could write about. First of all, he could write a report about the traits that wolves share with humans. He decides instead to write a report about conflicts between humans and wolves. He knows a little bit about it, but would like to learn more.

The next step requires you to generate questions about the topic and then figure out how to go about finding the answers. Where do you go to find some additional information about wolves? In this case the author can go to the library and look up wolves. Better yet, he can go to a zoo and talk to the people there. They should be able to tell him something and might even be able to give him the name of an expert. That sounds like a lot more fun than sitting in a library.

He also knows there are ranchers in the area. He finds a couple of names at the newspaper. It would be great to interview a rancher and find his or her feelings about wolves.

As you can see, there are lots of different ways to gather information for writing. Papers that result from sitting in a library and writing are not as interesting as papers written by an author who has gone out and really gotten involved with a topic. If you decide you need to use the library, you may want to start with the children's section. The books there are organized around the main ideas of the topic and help you to see the various ways the information can be organized.

If you are going to use some other methods for gathering information, such as interviews and field trips, you have to do a lot of careful planning. You need to establish a schedule and stick to it. Arrange your interviews well in advance. If you are going to write away for information, be sure to give the person you are writing to plenty of time to respond.

Keeping track of facts. Taking notes is very important as you gather information. Notes can be taken in your journal, or on separate note cards. You need to develop a system that works for you. It is very helpful to have a file folder or envelope to keep together all the information you are gathering. If you are doing interviews, you will want to have plenty of tapes and a tape recorder to take with you. It's hard to ask questions and take notes at the same time. By using a tape recorder, you can still be involved in the conversation and have a record to refer back to later. But if you record all that information, be sure you give yourself enough time later to listen to the tapes and copy what you need from them. Hours and hours of interviews that are locked up in tapes that you don't have time to review can turn into a nightmare.

Getting it together. Once you've collected enough information to answer all your questions about a topic, you're ready to begin organizing your materials. This is where you can use your mapping skills. Go back to your original cluster or do a new one. Refer to your notes and other materials to refresh your memory. Do you see some natural paragraphs or sections for your paper developing?

Now you need to decide what kind of paper you are going to write. Will it be a descriptive paper, a compare-and-contrast paper, a cause-and-effect paper, a step-by-step process paper? There are many books, including your English textbook, which discuss the different kinds of papers.

The first time around. You are probably more than ready to write by now. Your rough draft is a place to start putting things together. You need to remember a rough draft is just that — rough. Some people like to refer to the rough draft as a sloppy copy. Here are some rules for writing a rough draft.

- Write in pencil without your notes.
- Skip lines.
- Don't worry about punctuation, spelling, and grammar.
- Concentrate on getting your thoughts and information down.

Changes. *Revision* means to change meaning. During revision you can add or delete information or reorganize the order in which it appears.

Revision is probably the most difficult part of writing a paper after getting a topic. Revision literally means re-seeing with a critical eye what you've written. Revision is tough because it sometimes means getting rid of things you've spent a lot of time writing. It doesn't mean just looking for misspelled words and mistakes. In fact, these things shouldn't be addressed until after you have finished revising.

There are several strategies you can use for revision. The most effective is to have someone else read the paper and react to it. Be sure to ask them not to worry about mechanics, just content. Another way is to put the paper away for a few days. Just stick it in a drawer and forget about it. Before you sit down again and read it out loud,

Writing Guide Checklist

Directions: Consider the following questions as you revise your writing.

✓ - okay   0 - needs revision   ? - can't tell

Organization of Ideas

☐ Did you begin your paper with a clear topic sentence that tells the reader what to expect in the paper?

☐ Did you include enough details and examples to support statements you make in the paper?

☐ Did you weave sentences together so that the sequence seems logical and easy to follow?

Word Choice and Style

☐ Did you vary your choice of words so the same words are not used over and over again?

☐ Did you use words that accurately and precisely express what you wanted to say?

☐ Did you vary sentence length so your paper isn't choppy?

Usage, Punctuation, Spelling, References

☐ Did you check to see if all your sentences are complete?

☐ Did you punctuate sentences correctly?

☐ Did you use correct capitalization?

☐ Did you check words that you sometimes misspell?

☐ Did you reference sources correctly and consistently?

Comments:

do another cluster and write down some questions you would expect to be answered in a paper about that topic. Read your paper over and see if you answered those questions.

Help from a friend. Now it's time to start looking at spelling, grammar, and punctuation. It's a good idea to have someone, your mom or dad or a friend, check your spelling, grammar, and punctuation. It's very hard, if not impossible, to catch your own mistakes. Some proofreaders put a piece of card under each line as they read. Others start at the bottom right-hand corner of the paper and read it backwards.

The finale. When you are ready to prepare your final copy of the paper to hand in, be sure to check with the teacher for any instructions he or she might have for the way your paper should look.

Proofreaders' Marks

≡	Virginia smith	Capitalize a lower-case letter.
/	"Going To Norway"	Change a capital letter to lower case.
∧	"The Glove and the Lions"	Insert a word or phrase.
ℰ	"Rikki Tikki Tavii"	Delete (take out) one or more letters and close up the space.
∧	James Jones (n)	Insert a letter.
⊙	O Henry	Add a period.
∧	stories, poems, and novels	Add a comma.
∨	"Cat & the Weather"	Insert quotation marks.
∼	Brian's Song	Change the order of the letters.
¶	¶ "The Monkey's Paw" is a scary story.	Begin a new paragraph.

Remember . . .

Completing a writing project takes planning, research, writing, rewriting, and some help from friends. The writing process pulls together a series of events that must be completed in order to finalize a writing experience. Learning how to do it can be exciting and rewarding. Writing will be crucial for you to get your ideas across, not only in school, but throughout the rest of your life.

4

PREPsteps

Be prepared.

The Scout motto is always good advice, right?

And now that you're becoming an active learner, it's time to really learn how to prepare. PREPsteps will help you.

Each of the letters in PREP represents one of the four steps of the system. The letters and what they stand for are:

Previewing

Reading and studying actively

Examining

Prompting

The chart below explains the meaning of these words.

Previewing	getting an overall picture of the material you need to learn even before you start the job of learning it (You can use previewing in your reading assignments, various projects, and observations.)
Reading and Studying Actively	figuring out what information is important, recording that information in a notebook for later use, and forming questions a teacher might ask

Examining	being critical; learning to ask questions before you begin, during the lesson, and after you have finished
Prompting	using memory skills and techniques to help you recall the information — reciting out loud, for example, or asking yourself questions and answering them (The goal of prompting is to put new information into long-term storage in your brain so you can retrieve it as you need it, or to know where information is stored so you can retrieve it when you need it; for example, in your computer or your textbook.)

PREPsteps will help you learn more effectively. The skills involved in these steps include some that we've already discussed and some new ones:

- asking and making up questions
- organizing information
- writing summaries
- learning how to paraphrase
- checking out what you already know
- reviewing your work daily.

What are the pay-offs for being prepared? Most kids report more self-confidence, a sense of accomplishment, and work finished on time. Kids also report when they use the PREPsteps, they learn more, understand more fully what they're studying, put more information into long-term storage in the brain, and become more productive students. They also get better grades.

Now for the Coming Attractions: Previewing

Previewing helps you get ready to actively start or read an assignment. Getting ready to learn is the first step in the learning process. When applied to reading, previewing:

• helps serve as a warm-up for later, more careful reading
• helps you ask these questions: What do I think the story will be about? What do I already know about this topic? What do I want to know?
• helps you increase your understanding of the materials
• gives you an overview of what the material is about

Recalling information about the topic will help with your concentration. The information you already know is called prior knowledge. Associating new information with ideas that you have already learned is a major learning technique.

calling up prior knowledge	+	new information	=	more complete understanding of the idea or topic

There is one more advantage to previewing. It gets you actively involved. Previewing reduces mind wandering and daydreaming, which happens to lots of students as they study.

Previewing includes five steps.

1. *Examine the title.* Check out your prior knowledge. Ask yourself "What do I know about this title?" But be careful; sometimes the title isn't the topic.

2. *Read the introduction, and opening and closing paragraphs.* You should be able to determine the topic. Write the topic idea on a piece of paper, then take a little time — three to five minutes would be good — to write down anything you can think of about that topic. This is called creating a cluster.

3. *Review the major headings and subheadings.* These are often clues to the main ideas of a topic. Do the headings introduce the main ideas of this passage? Sometimes there are headings that are not main ideas. By now you

will have a good idea of what the author wants you to know. Let the summary guide you in decisions about main ideas.

4. *Examine all pictures, graphs, charts, and other visual aids.* Ask yourself, "What does the graphic tell me about this information?"

5. *Look at the questions throughout the chapter as well as at the end of the chapter.* Often the answers to these reveal the main ideas.

Now look at each step in more detail.

The title of the show. The title usually announces the topic to the reader. When you preview, ask yourself: What do I think the material will be about? What do I already know about the topic? What do I want to learn about the topic?

Then practice on the titles below. What do you think the following articles would be about if you were given these titles? Write a brief description for each title that follows.

Rattlesnakes _____

_____

Abe Lincoln Grows Up _____

_____

What You Can Do About Skin Problems _____

_____

Stars and Stellar Distances _____

_____

A Dog No Eyes Can See _____

_____

Which titles are you sure about? Why do you think so? Which ones gave you some problems? Why? We've provided descriptions of our own. Check them against yours to see how they compare.

The piece on rattlesnakes could be about where the snakes live, how they survive, and their place in the ecosystem.

The Abe Lincoln article might be about Abe as a young boy and the kinds of things he did then.

The skin problems article could provide information about skin care and some of the treatments that are available for different skin conditions.

The stars article could be about stellar distances and the various constellations found in the heavens.

The dog article might be about a seeing eye dog and how it becomes the eyes for a blind person.

Skip the introductions? Definitely not! The introduction is the author's first chance to communicate with the reader. Many authors use the opening paragraph to give you some information about the background of the piece you're about to read. They also give you some clues about the main ideas of the material.

Sometimes the author does not present a formal introduction statement. At this point you need to read the first and last paragraphs. Authors usually introduce the subject they will be writing about in the first paragraph and summarize their important ideas in the last paragraph.

Pretend you've picked up an article with the title "Cheetah: Earthbound Flier." The first and last paragraphs follow. Write three ideas you think might be included in the story before reading the paragraphs.

1. _____

_____

2. _____

_____

3. _____

_____

Now read the following paragraphs.

First paragraph:

The cheetah is a nonconformist by feline standards. Even its sleek appearance is astonishingly dog-like for a cat. With small rounded ears set wide apart, and long, slender legs that bring to mind a greyhound, the cheetah (Acinonyx jubatus) is so unusual among old world feline that it is classified in a separate subfamily (Acinonychinae). But the cheetah is, nonetheless, a cat and shares with its cousins a dubious future.

Last paragraph:

Though captive breeding must be carried on as insurance against the extinction of the species, man must focus his attention on preserving a free, wild population. By mandating greater protection and by implementing a good, captive breeding program, man might keep the African cheetah from joining its Asiatic cousins on the increasing rolls of nearly extinct animals.

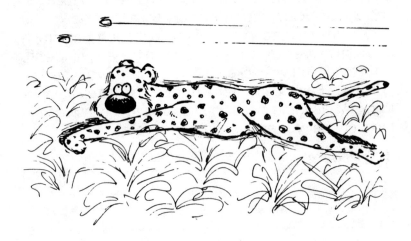

Did your ideas show up in the paragraphs? Did the title of the passage help you predict what might be in the two paragraphs? Do you think you can guess a lot of what will be in the overall story from having read the first and last paragraphs?

Sure you do. This is some special cat, after all.

An important pair of words from the first paragraph is the "dubious future" phrase. The phrase provides a clue that not only is the cheetah special, but it may be in trouble. That's confirmed in the last paragraph. It's in at least some danger of becoming extinct, and a lot has to be done to protect it. Now, knowing what you know about the cheetah and what to look for in the article, you can get all the details by reading the stuff in between — the meat in your knowledge sandwich. But you've already gotten a lot from the slices of bread on the outside — the title, and first and last paragraphs.

Using your head(ings). Survey the material quickly to locate the heading and subheadings. That will show you the author's plan for organizing the book, chapter, or article. For example, you may find that a textbook chapter is divided into three main ideas with three subheadings for each. This tells you to pay close attention to the three main ideas. By figuring out the author's plan, you've already begun to understand the ideas in the chapter even before you start your reading.

Just picture this. People have said that a good picture is worth a thousand words. This is particularly true in previewing. A graph, chart, or picture can tell you a great deal about the main ideas of the passage. The graphic can show a really complicated idea in picture form, making it easier for you to understand. So, don't pass up the illustrations in your previewing and when you read. Take time to look at them, read the captions around them, and use them to understand the new information.

A chart, like the one below, might be found in your health textbook.

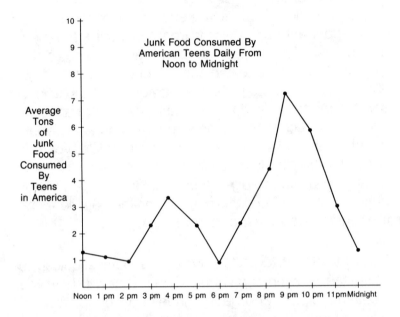

Source: The U.S. Junk Food Preservation Society

Questions first. Authors usually provide questions in textbooks. Some questions are found after each section of the chapter; some are presented at the end of the chapter; and at times the actual subheadings in the chapters are questions. By previewing the questions first, you ought to get an idea of what the author thinks is important. Use the questions as a guide to unlocking the meaning of the material. Make notes of them, and the answers will pop out at you as you read.

Questions at the end of a chapter in your health book might include the following.

- *What are the basic food groups?*
- *How much fat should you eat each day?*
- *What's the most popular time for children to eat junk food?*
- *Why is it important for children to drink milk?*
- *How can the labels on food products help you make healthy choices about what to buy?*

◤ Remember . . .

Previewing, the first of our four PREPsteps, is a strategy you can use for getting prepared to read. Following the previewing methods we've given will tell you a lot about what's in the article or chapter before you even begin. Now you can go on to really reading — that is, actively reading — the chapter.

Let's Get Hyper: Reading and Studying Actively

We introduced you to active reading in Chapter Two. Now it's time for more detailed information to describe our second PREPstep.

You become totally involved with the material when you read actively. You also approach different types of reading in different ways, depending on its content as well as your purpose for reading. In courses such as geography, science, civics, home economics, math, or language arts, you're more likely to recall the important information later if you read actively.

The steps to active reading and studying are:

- Read flexibly.
- Find the topic, main ideas, and details.
- Learn to separate topic, main ideas, and details.
- Take notes for later study, writing summary statements and mapping the material.

An English teacher once said to the class as he got ready to read a story:

> *If you want to understand a book, you must live it. You must feel the rain on your face, the warmth from the sun, the joy, sadness, and frustrations described in the story.*

He wanted his students to become a part of what they were reading rather than just reading the words. How much you become involved in what you read depends on your interest, purpose in reading, and willingness to become involved.

A real reading workout: read flexibly. An active reader is also a flexible reader; someone who realizes that all materials are not read at the same rate. There are four main factors that determine how fast you should read any kind of reading material:

- the difficulty of the material
- your purpose in reading
- the writer's purpose
- how much you know about a topic.

It isn't so difficult to understand that some materials are just harder to read than others. A comic book isn't as tough as a math book. You read a magazine differently than a novel. You might find a science textbook harder to understand than your social studies book. Each reading task may also have a different purpose. If you're a flexible reader, you'll be able to adjust and choose a reading rate according to the difficulty of the material and the purpose for reading.

The hunt is on: find the topic, main ideas, and details. Identify the topic. Ask yourself: What is the one major idea in the whole passage or lecture? Sometimes you'll have to preview material you're reading to answer the question. Other times the topic is announced in the title. But watch out for eye-catching titles that don't give you a clue about the topic. *The Color Purple* by Alice Walker is not a book about coloring or painting, and *Coming Up for Air* by George Orwell is not about deep-sea diving. So don't be fooled.

Now try your hand at finding the topic.

Here are lists of ideas that could be topics, main ideas, or details. Circle the word in each list that is the topic.

1. baseball
   interscholastic sports
   junior varsity teams
   football

2. taking notes
   math test
   class discussion
   school work

3. music
   laser discs
   Rock and Roll
   classical music

4. New York City
   Pennsylvania
   United States of America
   The County of Los Angeles

See bottom of page for answers

Your answers should be? 1. Interscholastic sports;
2. school work; 3. music; 4. United States of America
How did you do?

Once you have identified the topic, you can begin your search for the main ideas. There are usually several main ideas organized around a topic. The topic is the broadest and details are the narrowest levels of information. Use the lists above as practice in figuring out which is which.

Now it's time to find the details. Details often answer the questions: Who? When? Where? They always help you understand the main ideas better.

Details should be expressed in words and phrases. Details must help you complete your understanding of the main ideas. If they don't make the idea clearer in your mind, they are unnecessary or trivial.

You can think of the three levels of information as a cherry pie. There's the whole pie, piping hot from the oven, smelling wonderful and making you hungry. Then there are the slices of the pie. You're ready to dig in. And finally, there are the cherries inside your piece of pie, sweet and delicious.

It's the same with an information pie. First, you have the pie — the topic of the article, the big picture. Then there are the main ideas — each of the slices. Finally, there are the details, each one a sweet nugget of information that helps to tell about the main ideas.

All of the information pie is important, and it's important for you to recognize whether you're looking at the pie, the slices, or the cherries in the slices. Don't confuse the topic with the main ideas. The topic is what the entire article or lecture is about and can be very broad. The main ideas are the major points that make up the topic. Main ideas usually answer questions that begin with *what*, *why*, and *how*. They can describe, define, compare, explain, and summarize too, so keep those terms in mind when you're trying to figure out the main ideas, and while you separate them from the more general topic.

Sometimes it's harder to figure out which is the whole pie and which are the pieces when you're listening to a lecture rather than reading from a book. After all, unless you're taping it, you can't listen over and over again to what was said the way you can reread a passage in a book. You don't usually have visual clues, such as chapter headings and titles, and you can't really preview the teacher's lesson the same as you would a chapter in your text. But you can focus on the speaker. Try to eliminate distractions, and listen carefully. Speakers sometimes stray from their topics. Learn to recognize when this occurs.

Listen first; then write. Be selective about what you write. Use terms, key words, and phrases. Don't attempt to write whole sentences. Don't try to write down everything the speaker is saying. This is impossible. Write down complete thoughts about the important information presented, but not every word. And remember, it's a good rule to copy down everything the speaker writes on the board or shows on a transparency. And don't forget to ask questions. If you're uncertain about an idea or if you think you've missed something, ask about it.

The supporting cast: learn to separate topic, main ideas, and details. Information comes in all shapes and sizes — from gigantic to miniscule, often in a jumble. You need to unjumble the mess, or organize

it. One way of doing that is by categorizing each piece of information you get as a topic, a main idea, or a detail. Then patterns can emerge and you can finally begin to make sense of it.

Think of a pyramid turned on its point. The topic is on top, the main ideas under it, with details getting smaller and smaller as they go down.

Let's look at an example.

Here are four pieces of related information:

books   *Winnie the Pooh*   **children's books**   **Eeyore**

Which is the broadest piece of information? Which is the narrowest? The topic "books" is the largest of the four choices. Children's books are a kind of book classification and *Winnie the Pooh* is the title of a children's book. It is a narrower piece of information than children's books. Eeyore, the donkey, is a character in *Winnie the Pooh* and therefore the narrowest of all four pieces of information.

Getting it down: take notes for later study. Your notes are your deep freeze. They'll keep information fresh until you need it. They also are your means of organizing material so you understand it. Good notes will help you study for tests and really learn what you've covered, with the information moving into long-term storage in your brain. In Chapter Five we will show you three methods of note-taking, with each providing a strong system that will last through your learning years. You'll learn how to write summary statements that will crystallize the most important information into knowledge ice cubes that will thaw as you need them. You will learn how to draw a study map, a visual aid to memory that will help you organize for tests. You can even draw information maps as you take tests, or as you plan big writing projects.

⚡Remember . . .

Active reading and studying, the second PREPstep, requires you to be involved with what you read. Remember your information pie — topic, main ideas, and details. The pie will help you organize the material into a meaningful record. To help you find the topic, main ideas, and details don't forget to

- preview.
- use visual clues like boldface print and graphics.
- reread material.
- read the summary.
- examine the book's questions.
- read with a pencil to record your impressions as you go.
- take good notes.

Elementary, My Dear Watson: Examining

The third of our PREPsteps — examining, or asking questions — goes hand in hand with active reading. Smart learners ask questions **before**, **during**, and **after** reading, listening, and observing. Smart learners also ask different kinds of questions depending on the purpose of the question. Asking questions helps smart learners identify what's worth learning.

Books, people, and events are storehouses of information. What you want to be able to do is transfer that information from the material to long-term storage inside your head. In order to understand the material you'll need to ask lots of questions. Try to include in your questions the sort your teacher might ask. You know the kind. In history, for example, you might ask when Lincoln issued the Emancipation Proclamation that freed the slaves. Your teacher, on the other hand, might ask you to write an essay on the part that slavery played in starting the Civil War.

These will help you think about the material you're try-ing to learn. And you'll find that as you draw up ques-tions from the material, you'll often be able to answer them from the same source — the material itself.

There are three kinds of questions an active reader should ask:

1. *Questions of fact* ask you to recall something the au-thor said, either in your own words or by reading a pas-sage from the selection. These questions depend on memory and have only one right answer. What makes a statement a fact is not whether you believe it but that the author said it. A fact question can usually be answered by holding your hand over your mouth and pointing to the answer. It doesn't require an explanation.

2. *Questions of interpretation* ask you for your opinion about the author's meaning. Answers to these questions depend on more than just memory. The author doesn't usually explain why certain ideas appear in the selection. The author hasn't written the words you need for your an-swer, but you must decide the meaning yourself. For ex-ample, a book about nature could paint a savage picture of predator and prey. Or as in *The Call of the Wild*, it can make nature appear to be connected with human choices and values. You might decide from reading it that the au-thor thinks nature closely connects wild animals with man, although he never actually says so in the book. Such a conclusion would be your opinion, and since there's a gap between your opinion and what the author actually writes, you can't be certain you're correct. A question of interpre-tation requires that you explain your answer by using evi-dence from the selection. Someone may disagree based on different evidence from the same piece.

3. *Questions of evaluation* ask you whether you agree or disagree with the author's meaning on the basis of what you already know. In these answers you talk about your-self as you give reasons. Don't rely on words like *what* or *why* to help you. "What do you think?" is tricky. "Why?"

can be a fact question or an interpretation question, depending on the answer you seek. The best test to determine the kind of question you are answering is to try to answer it for thirty seconds. If your answer is coming from within the reading, it is either factual or interpretative. If you can cover your mouth and point to the answer, it is factual. If your answer is coming from your experience, it is evaluative.

When to ask when, *and other questions.* Ques-
tions can be made up before, while, and after reading, listening, and observing. You become an active participant through your questions. If you ask questions during the history lesson, your history teacher would probably describe you as active, not a wallflower or a sleeper. Your questions have made you an active participant. It's the same when you are studying on your own. It isn't simply to gain a few brownie points from the teacher that you're asking all those questions. They help you to really understand the material — and you need to ask them whether they're directed to your teacher or to yourself. It's especially important to ask questions that cover the main ideas — that is, the important information.

The kinds of questions you ask depend on the levels of information you need to remember.

. . . at the detail level, ask questions that are used to describe something, some detail, about a main idea.

Where did the Oregon Trail begin and end?

How long does it take the liver to break down the alcohol contained in an average drink?

What is one way water can be purified?

When was Martin Luther King assassinated?

Who took the first step on the moon?

. . . at the main idea level, ask questions about the main ideas and the topic.

> **Why do eagles remain in the same habitat throughout their lifetimes?**
>
> **How do political parties select their presidential candidates?**
>
> **Why are observations important to discoveries in science?**
>
> **What are the symptoms of AIDS?**

Questions require answers. Answers require action. As you create teacher-type questions, you are becoming a smart learner.

How do you get started asking questions? Per-

haps the best way to learn to ask questions is to make a game of it. The TV show *Jeopardy* has the right idea. During the game answers are provided, and players must supply a question to match the answers. It's not as easy as you might think.

Suppose you were given the answer *nine*. Beyond the automatic math questions such as: What is three times three? and What is six plus three? there are questions from literature, sports, and almost any other subject area that could have the answer nine.

How many men are on a baseball team?

How many innings are in a baseball game?

How many lives does a cat have?

How many pounds did John Henry's hammer weigh?

How many symphonies did Beethoven compose?

Playing *Jeopardy* is a good way to prepare for tests. Take 25 key ideas or terms and make them into questions. You will know when you're ready for the test when you can answer all the questions.

Now you've got the (main) idea. There are several ways to form main-idea questions.

- Change the subheadings in textbooks or articles into questions.
- Use questions in the chapter if the author provides them.
- Write questions that use the words *why, what, how,* and *describe.*

Usually there will be one question for each main idea. In order to create a question about a main idea and its details, you must understand the information. You need to think about the information in your notes. What is the idea being presented? Develop one question that pulls that information together.

To help you get started, look at the series of questions below. These examples will show you what main idea questions look like in science, math, social studies, health, and English.

Science Questions

How are the functions of muscles and bones related?

What causes the different phases of the moon?

What does *biodegradable* mean?

Social Studies Questions

What is a ghetto?

Why are the harbors and waterways of the Middle Atlantic states so important to that part of the country's economic future?

How does the impeachment process work in the federal government?

Language Arts Questions

What is the conflict in the story?

What is the final outcome?

What is the story's theme or main idea?

Mathematics Questions

What two whole numbers are neither prime nor composite? Why is this true?

What is a positive integer?

Why is the use of estimation important?

Health Questions

What are some ways people avoid health problems?

Why is water important to your health?

How would you administer CPR?

Remember . . .

Using questions is one way to focus on the information to be learned. Asking, writing, and answering questions will help you remember what's important. Questions are the most important way to understand what you read and hear.

Heating Up Cold Storage: Prompting

Prompting, the last of our four PREPsteps, helps you remember information. It is a skill that will help you find and retrieve information, images, and feelings from your brain and other sources.

Psychologists have discovered that the human brain never loses anything. What we call forgetting is really our inability to retrieve information stored in our brains, or our failure to store the information in our long-term storage in the first place. The suggestions presented in this chapter will help you do a better job of storing and retrieving information you want to remember.

Reaching into the freezer. There are several things you can do to prompt yourself to remember material you want to learn and retain.

- *Decide you want to remember the material.* Concentrate while you read and study.
- *Apply what you are learning in your daily life.* Ask yourself: How can I use this information? When you use information all the time, you won't forget it.
- *Organize the information* you want to learn.
- *Create a list of questions* about the information and answer the questions.
- *Recite what you are trying to learn.* Reading out loud, to yourself or to your study group (more about that later), is one of the most powerful memory aids.
- *Explain the new information to a friend.* If you can talk about it, you know it.
- *Discuss the main ideas* and other important points in a group discussion.
- *Schedule your learning sessions.* Don't wait until the last minute to study. Space several short sessions over a period of time.
- *Overlearn the material.* Study until the information is part of you.

The big bonus. Memory is more than a tool to be used in school. Now more than ever before, the ability to recall information is an essential job skill. The information explosion is affecting all fields of work. The amount of information you will have to know just to hold a job in the future is staggering. Right now information is increasing at a rate of 15% per year. That rate is expected to increase to more than 30% a year in the next decade. This means the information that's available will double every two to three years. You will need a system that enables you to handle all the information that will bombard you.

People who are able to devise such a system, one that prompts memories buried deep in long-term storage back to consciousness, will do well. An effective memory will assist you in finding the links between what you already know and what's new.

Togetherness — it pays off. Study with others is energizing. Learning and thinking are social activities. Besides the support and fun you can have, the study group can encourage you and make you work harder. You can also help other members when they need it.

When forming your study group, find people whom you're comfortable with and who share your academic goals. The challenge of forming a good study group is in asking others like yourself to participate and in setting rules you will live by. Limit your group to four people. When working in a group, use the following guidelines:

- *Test each other by asking questions.* Group members should practice predicting test questions.
- *Teach each other.* It's often been said that the best way to learn something is to adopt a positive attitude that says: I know this. The more you talk about it the better you know it.
- *Compare notes.* Make sure you all recorded the same important information. Discuss information that may confuse you.
- *Brainstorm possible test questions.* Write them down for future reference and study.
- *Discuss ideas.* This will help to make sense of the information to be learned.
- *Draw a diagram to help you remember.* Such a diagram, complete with labels, road signs, and arrows to important ideas is called a group study map. We'll show you how to make maps in Chapter Five.

Studying in groups pays off. Collective thinking is always better than thinking just on your own. So cooperate with some of your fellow classmates and form a study group today.

Remember . . .

One of the goals in learning is to retain as much information as possible in long-term memory storage. You must learn to prompt your memory to take important information and then to call it up on command, just like a computer would. Your mind is the best computer in the world.

It is far superior to the most complex electronic hardware. You simply need to develop the software — the methods we've described — to make the most out of what you have.

5

Take Note

In this chapter we discuss three methods of notemaking. We've got our own little code words for them — î notes, mapping, and SSS.

Notice we said "notemaking", not "notetaking." We think there is a difference. It is the difference between learning actively and learning passively. Notemakers control what goes with their notes. They don't just copy words. They read or listen — then think — before they write. Notemakers are decision-makers. They are disciplined — they select a helpful notemaking format, and they write only the important, useful information.

Me, Myself and î

The ninth letter in the alphabet is an î. Think of the shape of the lower case î. It has the dot at the top and a long skinny stroke, a single straight line that sort of hangs down from the dot.

Looking at the î that way — The dot at the top with the rest hanging on below — can help you remember the î note method. Making an î note begins with an actual drawing of a large î, with a circle for the dot and a long rectangle below.

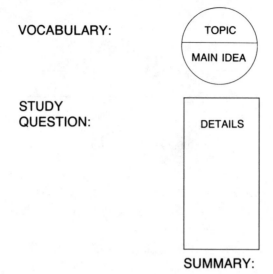

VOCABULARY: TOPIC

                                   MAIN IDEA

STUDY
QUESTION: DETAILS

                                   SUMMARY:

In the circle will go the topic and main idea, with details filling the box below. Just below the ▯, leave space
for a summary of your notes. Just outside the ▯ on the
left, leave space for at least one main idea question, and
in the top left, draw up a short list of new vocabulary
you've encountered.

When you write ▯ notes you record the most important
points in the reading or lecture — the topic and the main
idea — right at the top. But remember, to be complete,
an ▯ note has six parts: the topic, main idea, details, summary, main idea questions, and vocabulary list.

Here's how to make sure you have them all:

- Preview the material. Determine the topic.
- Read actively, listing new vocabulary as you go. Dis-
  cover the main ideas.
- Select the important details that describe the main ideas.
- Write a summary. Restate the major ideas in your own
  words.
- Write at least one main-idea question.

As you build your ℹ, try to use as few words as possible, and abbreviate where you can. The less you have to plow through during review, the easier it will be for you. But make sure the information is complete and you understand it. In listing details, get rid of words that are mentioned in the topic and main ideas. Use a shorthand system for common words. Write only key words. Use as many as you need to keep the meaning. Keep it lean, but remember this is your system to retrieve information when you need it. If you cannot tell somebody about the material as you scan your ℹ notes, you haven't put enough information down. At first, you'll probably cram lots of information into each ℹ, but as you get better at it, you'll use fewer and fewer words.

Writing a summary is the best way to see if you have a complete understanding of the main idea. In writing a summary, you want to restate the main idea in one sentence. Don't include details in your summary. Remember, you want to rewrite the main idea of this ℹ.

How do you write main-idea questions? In Chapter Four you learned how to write various types of questions. One type was the main-idea question. Look back over that section (pages 49-54) to refresh your memory. From now on, we'll be asking you to write main-idea questions, so get the format down pat. Remember, they begin with words like *what, how, why, describe, define, compare,* and *show.*

An example of a main-idea question taken from the passage above is: *What tells desert animals it's time to come out of their burrows?*

How many î notes should be written for a topic? Limit yourself to no more than seven main ideas for one topic, with the fewer you must build the better. However, you must make sure you have all the necessary information for the topic on which you are working. So, don't leave anything out. Below is an article on newspapering, with an accompanying series of î notes.

Read the article, "What Is a Newspaper?" As you read it, ask yourself these questions:

1. What is the topic?
2. What are the main ideas?
3. What are three details that support each main idea?

⚡Remember . . .

There are three levels of information: topics, main ideas, and details. The î notes you write help you organize information into six parts: topic, main idea, details, summary, main idea questions, and vocabulary. Your î notes are helpful when you need to analyze difficult pieces of information. Now review the completed "î's" on "What Is a Newspaper?" Do you agree?

What Is a Newspaper?

The Random House Dictionary of the English Language defines 'news' as 'a report of a recent event' or 'a report on current events in a newspaper or on radio or television.' A newspaper is defined as 'a publication, usually issued daily or weekly, containing news comment, features, photographs and advertising.'

The dictionary definition of news, however, leaves much to be desired in the context of newspapering, because much of any newspaper's content has nothing to do with reports of recent events. For example, the crossword puzzle that is a staple in many newspapers and the first thing some readers turn to hardly qualifies as news. The same is true of comics. These are features, and in most newspapers they occupy greater space than news. Perhaps a newspaper should be called a 'news and feature paper.'

Newspapers also contain advertising, and the accepted ratio of news to advertisements is 60 percent ads, 40 percent news. So maybe a newspaper should be called an 'adpaper.'

There is really much more to the modern newspaper than reports of recent events. Some of this can be traced to the *Acta Diurna* of Roman times when daily bulletins were posted on walls for everyone to read. Diurna means daily and these daily bulletins established one of the standards of a newspaper: regular, consistent publication. Six centuries later, the Chinese Tsing-Pao began a long period of publishing, lasting until this century.

Freedom of the Press

But the roots of modern newspapers really lay in Europe in somewhat more recent times. Although there were brief attempts at publishing on the continent during the 17th century, it was in England that the newspaper really took root. William Caxton, a printer, is credited with the first examples. But many freedoms were lost under the autocracy of Henry VIII and subsequent rules, and freedom of the press was one of them.

It was largely because of such oppression that America was founded, and it wasn't long before printers in the American colonies — Benjamin Harris in Massachusetts and Benjamin Franklin in Philadelphia — began using their presses to speak out against curbs on individual freedoms. Thus early newspapers were not as much reports of recent events as examples of what have come to be known today as expressions of editorial opinion.

What constitutes a "newspaper?" Here are some of the commonly accepted characteristics:

- It must be published at regular intervals. Daily newspapers appear every day, weeklies every week. Some community newspapers appear at less-frequent intervals; nevertheless, they appear consistently and continuously.
- It must be devoted to the masses. In other words, it must contain general, not specialized, information, although it may have specialty sections with information that doesn't interest every reader, such as sports or food.
- It must be available to everyone who wants it, and not to a select few.
- It must contain news. That means according to the Random House dictionary, reports on 'current events.'
- It must champion the interests of its geographic constituency. That means that a newspaper in New York should contain news of New York, not Philadelphia, for the most part. But geographic constituency can be narrowly defined. The *Village Voice* was created to serve the interests of residents of New York's Greenwich Village, for example.

One big way in which a newspaper differs from a news magazine is in its geographical constituency. Magazines may carry news, but their geographical constituency is the entire nation; most newspapers have a more narrow geographical focus. An exception is *USA Today* which is something like a national news-magazine (i.e., *Time* or *Newsweek*) and is printed on newsprint at plants in Atlanta, Minneapolis, St. Paul, Chicago, Denver, Houston, Los Angeles, Miami, New York, Philadelphia, and Washington with new locations added as the paper grows.

Legal Definition

There are also legal definitions of a newspaper. The State of Maryland, for example, has defined a newspaper in very specific terms. Article 81 of the Annotated Code of Maryland states that a publication isn't a newspaper unless:

- it is published and distributed no less frequently than once each week
- it does not, when its successive issues are put together, constitute a book
- it is intended for circulation among the general public
- it contains news items, legal and general intelligence, reports of current events, editorial comments, advertising matter, and other miscellaneous items of public interest generally found in the ordinary newspaper.

The definition of what a newspaper is really lies in the uses to which it will be put. Every big newspaper of substance tries to keep its readers informed on events that concern them. Part of that elusive equality called 'editorial judgment' is the ability of the art of its editors to feel, almost instinctively, what is news and what isn't. Press releases by the millions, pour through the mails to the editorial officers of newspapers around the world. Many are boldly headlined NEWS. To some people they are, but an editor must decide if they are news to the readers of a specific newspaper.

Many editors of metropolitan newspapers consider themselves historians. Laboring with a sense of history borne of long hours of editing the day's news, they know that in future years, scholars will pour over microfilmed records of a specific period. This seemed especially to be the case of the *Washington Star*, no longer published. Headlines from this famous newspaper, once the nation's leading chronicle of U.S. government actions, read like a history book: 'War Declared on Axis'; 'Europe Invaded'; 'War Ends'; 'Russia Launches Sputnik'; 'JFK Dies of Gunshot Wound'; 'Nixon Resigns' — headlines like these are like pages of American history. It's all there, in newspapers.

From: Ronald Lovell and Phillip Ceract: THE MODERN MASS MEDIA MACHINE, ©1987 by Kendall/Hunt Publishing Company. Reprinted by permission.

Vocabulary:

publication
feature

Topic:

newspaper

Main idea:

history / development

Study Question(s):

How have
newspapers
evolved?

Details:

Ancient:
        root of newspapers - Acta Diurna
            (daily bulletin)
        Long period of publishing -
            Chinese - Tsing Pao

Modern:
        17th century - roots of modern press
        Wm. Caxton - 1st English printer
        Henry VIII crushed freedom of the
            press
        America - Harris & Franklin were
            editors who promoted
            individual freedoms

Summary:

The simple daily bulletin has evolved into a
complex source of information.

Vocabulary:

intervals

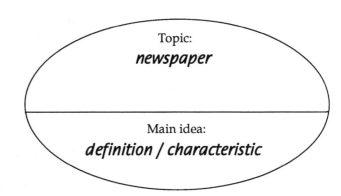

Topic:
newspaper

Main idea:
definition / characteristic

Study Question(s):

What is a newspaper?

What are the basic characteristics of a newspaper?

Details:
Definition:
Published regularly
contains general information
available to all
reports on current, local events
Characteristics:
news, ads, crossword puzzle,
comics, advice, editorials,
headlines
news / ad ratio is 40/60
(usually)

Summary:

The modern newspaper is a collection of current news and features distributed on a regular basis.

Vocabulary:

censorship
editorial

Topic:

newspaper

Main idea:

impact of newspapers

Study Question(s):

What is the impact of newspapers on the public?

Details:

- *promote awareness of current developments*
- *increase importance of reading*
- *freedom of the press v. censorship (started with Henry VIII)*
- *help settle America*
- *influence public opinion (editorials)*
- *alternative form of historical record*

Summary:

Newspapers give information; change opinion and record history.

Mapping Your Thoughts

Mapping is the second method of notemaking that you can use to organize information. Mapping is a picture of information. It contains all the important information on a topic condensed to one page. You can use mapping for lectures, reading assignments, and observations or all three together. Through mapping, you will understand the relationship of the levels of information (topic, its main ideas, details) and have a better chance of retrieving data when you need it.

What is mapping? Mapping resembles a road map. A road map shows you a scaled-down picture of an area. It provides an overview of the land and it points out the major routes.

A map of your school work is the same thing. It gives you, in picture form and on one page, a scaled-down picture of the important information of a lesson or unit. What you read, hear, or observe can be organized in one place.

There are five major steps in mapping:

- Determine the topic.
- Create and organize the main idea.
- List the important details under each main idea.
- Write a summary.
- Create two kinds of questions.

How do you get started? What does mapping look like? Imagine that you have just taken a hard look at television and its impact on people. You've read a study and collected lots of information. You decide to make a map on this topic.

Your map should include the following:

- information organized by topic, main ideas, and details
- a summary
- main-idea questions
- higher-level questions

Your TV map might look like this:

Impact of Television

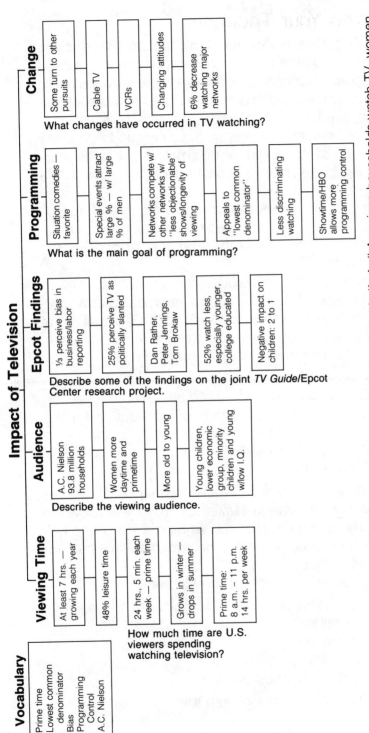

Vocabulary

Prime time
Lowest common
denominator
Bias
Programming
Control
A.C. Nielson

Viewing Time

At least 7 hrs. —
growing each year

48% leisure time

24 hrs., 5 min. each
week — prime time

Grows in winter —
drops in summer

Prime time:
8 a.m. – 11 p.m.
14 hrs. per week

How much time are U.S.
viewers spending
watching television?

Audience

A.C. Nielson
93.8 million
households

Women more
daytime and
primetime

More old to young

Young children,
lower economic
group, minority
children and young
w/low I.Q.

Describe the viewing audience.

Epcot Findings

1/3 perceive bias in
business/labor
reporting

25% perceive TV as
politically slanted

Dan Rather,
Peter Jennings,
Tom Brokaw

52% watch less,
especially younger,
college educated

Negative impact on
children: 2 to 1

Describe some of the findings on the joint *TV Guide*/Epcot
Center research project.

Programming

Situation comedies —
favorite

Special events attract
large % — w/ large
% of men

Networks compete w/
other networks w/
"less objectionable"
shows/longevity of
viewing

Appeals to
"lowest common
denominator"

Less discriminating
watching

Showtime/HBO
allows more
programming control

What is the main goal of programming?

Change

Some turn to other
pursuits

Cable TV

VCRs

Changing attitudes

6% decrease
watching major
networks

What changes have occurred in TV watching?

Summary: Television viewing time appears to be on the rise while almost half of all American households watch TV, women watch more TV at any time than men. Programming is a tactical business, bidding for viewers in a number of ways. Like anything else, change is occurring in the television industry. In an attempt to gain insight into TV viewing, *TV Guide* and Epcot Center teamed together and questioned viewers.

Higher Level Questions:
1) How might TV programmers better attract the interests of *both* the "typical" viewer and the more discriminating viewer?
2) Why is it that situation comedy enjoys so much popularity over and above all other programming?

What do you see? Can you find the topic? The main ideas? The details? Are there main-idea questions? Does the summary make sense? What are higher-level questions? Look at the example as you read the steps below. The numbers in parentheses indicate the step in which the information was added.

(1) Preview the material. Identify the topic. Write it in your notebook. In our example, you are investigating the impact of television, and you've done a lot of work already.

(2) Brainstorm to see what you know about the topic. Make a cluster by first writing down the topic, then brainstorm for three minutes or so, remembering all you can about it and writing it all down. Don't build the cluster on your map sheet, but keep it handy for when you're drawing the map.

(3) Select the main ideas. Organize the information you have gathered from different sources around the topic. Our map has five main idea areas: viewing time; audience; programming; change and Epcot findings.

(4) Attach the important details to each of the main ideas. Details can be vocabulary words, problems, equations, graphics, models, and examples. As you see from the example, programming details include the fact that situation comedies are audience favorites, that network TV must appeal to a "lowest common denominator" audience, and several more.

(5) Write a summary. The summary is a written statement of the main ideas on the map. As you see, the summary is written from the five main-idea boxes.

(6) Develop main-idea questions. Main-idea questions are placed next to each main idea and its details. You might want to use a colored pencil or pen for your

questions. One main-idea question you might have about programming is the one we've listed on our map.

Next, write questions that link the main ideas together, the kind that ask you to compare, analyze, create, develop, illustrate, and so forth.

(7) Remember to put specific terms in the upper left side of your map under the heading vocabulary. This will help you check whether you've included all the key ideas in the map.

You can highlight various parts of the map if you use certain symbols such as arrows, geometric shapes, and figures. It also helps to use color. Be as creative as you can. Mapping helps you see how information fits together. The ideas shown on the next page may help you.

Mapping Symbols
Used to Show the Relationship
Among Ideas on Maps

 Arrows — Show how concepts of a pattern are connected. Arrows can be single or multiheaded and can show backward and forward directions.

 Codes — Asterisks, exclamation marks, question marks, and other symbols show connection and add emphasis.

 Geometrical Shapes — Squares, oblongs, circles and ellipses mark words which are similar in nature and show order of importance.

 Artistic Three Dimension Objects — These 3-D figures show items of greater significance by making ideas "stand off" the page.

 Creativity/Images — Creativity can be combined with the use of dimension by making aspects of the pattern fit the topic.

 Color — Color enhances memory and creativity. Color can be used to show distinctions among ideas and also show relationship.

Your summary should:

- contain only the main ideas of the passage.
- be clear and easy to understand.
- not contain any ideas that are not in the passage or lesson.
- be written in your own words as much as possible.

Read the short passage and summary below. After you read the summary, examine it. Does it have the characteristics of a good summary?

Desert Animals

Nowhere in the world does **sundown release so many animals from burrows** as in a desert. Since early morning they have sought subterranean refuge from the burning glare. In twilight and darkness they emerge, **detecting** promptly **the time when**, through the clear air, **the soil's surface has radiated to space enough of the excessive daytime heat**. Their well-guarded **store of water** no longer is in such peril. Each can seek to supplement its energy supply, to **find** its favorite **food**.

Every desert-dwelling **animal** has some artful dodge whereby it **can exist without water** from one year's end to the next. A few, like snails and frogs, wait under-ground not only from dawn to dusk, but from one rain to the next, though the rains be a year apart. The rest **depend on some special means for getting water**. Most take it second hand from storage reservoirs of plants. Others manufacture the simple essential water molecule from atoms gained in dry foods. Some subsist on smaller animals which have these special abilities.

Summary

Sundown is the time when desert animals leave their burrows. They detect a cooling of the earth as the signal to come out. Desert animals learn to live without food and water for long periods of time. All desert animals and plants have learned special tricks to survive in the desert.

Once you've learned how to map, you have a second powerful way of making notes. Share your maps with classmates. Compare the way you organize information with how they do. Discuss what you agree on; that information is probably the most important to remember.

Discuss what you disagree on, too. That information also is important. You might want to reread your notes or parts of your textbook to come to an agreement with the kids in your group.

Finally, do a group map. Include possible test questions as well as key vocabulary.

⚡Remember . . .

Mapping is a way to organize information for later use. It gives you an opportunity to see how the different ideas of your assignment or reading fit together. Mapping can be used as a final step in preparing your material for study. It will give you a picture of the material you want to learn.

Splitting the Page:
SSS (Split-Summary System)

SSS is an organized way of recording information for later study. As we said earlier in the book, recording information is one way to become an active reader. And following an organized format is a way to active notemaking.

You probably already take notes, but you are probably not using any real method. You may be including too much trivial information or trying to write every word the teacher says. You may not have a way of showing which notes are the main ideas and which are the details. You may not have used highlighting, speed writing, or a shorthand system. Your notes may even become cold because you don't know what to do with them after class.

You've learned how to take ⓘ notes, and how to do mapping. SSS is a third way to takes notes. These three methods of notemaking are systematic. They will enable you to write down and remember the important things that you read or listen to. They will also give you a place to put each important notemaking ingredient. Knowing three methods will give you greater flexibility when you study. They probably will also give you better grades with less work.

How does SSS work? SSS consists of these parts:

- splitting the page into a notemaking column for class and textbook notes and a recall column for main idea questions and new vocabulary terms
- a summary.

SSS begins by dividing the paper into two columns: the recall column and the notemaking column. Look at the example below. Notice that the recall column is 2½'' wide. The notemaking column is approximately 6'' wide. You will have to draw a line on notebook paper to make these columns. The page looks like this:

RECALL	NOTES FROM THE READING OR LECTURE
	SUMMARY

Making It Work

The space is narrow, so some short cuts — like abbreviations and symbols — will be necessary.

Should you use abbreviations? Notes need to be an accurate record of information. Ways to shorten your notes are helpful as long as you can read and understand them later. There are several ways to use abbreviations. We recommend taking a course in Gregg shorthand if it is available. If not, buy a book on speedwriting and learn the system. This will help you save time and space in the long run.

- **Include only useful and important information.**
  For example, the following sentence:

  The people have a right to clean air, pure water, and to the preservation of the natural, scenic, historic, and aesthetic values of the environment.

  could be shortened to:

  People have rights to clean air, pure water, and beautiful country.

- **Use symbols whenever possible.**
  Here are some common symbols:

=	equal	≠	unequal
e.g.	for example	i.e.	in other words
&	and	>	greater than
<	less than	etc.	and so forth
@	at	#	number
$	dollar	%	percentage
÷	divided by		

- **Abbreviate words whenever possible.**
  Here are some common abbreviations:

biology	bio	history	hist
chemistry	chem	home economics	home ec
education	educ	dollar sign	$
United States	USA	nickel	5¢
extraterrestrial	ET	Los Angeles	LA

- **Leave out unnecessary words.**
  For example, the following sentence:

  Too often notes are written and ignored until weeks later when test time is close.

  could be shortened to:

  Notes are ignored until test time.

How should you use SSS? Notes are recorded on the right 6″ column of the page. Abbreviations should be used whenever possible. When using this system, traditional outlining that uses numbers or letters is not usually necessary unless the speaker gives you specific directions. Instead, categorize levels of information — topic, main ideas, and details — by indenting and spacing.

THE SUMMARY SHEET SYSTEM

RECALL	NOTES
The following activities belong here:	Record lecture notes here. These should be indented in this manner.
• Questions about main ideas	*Topic*
• Questions that need to be clarified by the teacher	*Main Idea 1* *Detail 1* *Detail 2* *Detail 3*
• Possible test questions	*Detail 4*
• Key words, formulas, and definitions	*Main Idea 2* *Detail 1* *Detail 2* *Detail 3* *Detail 4*
When using this column:	*Main Idea 3* *Detail 1*
RECITE	*Detail 2* *Detail 3*
REVIEW	*Detail 4*
REFLECT	*Summary*

What goes in the recall column? The recall column is the 2½" space. The purpose of the recall column is to provide thinking space on the information, to predict test questions, and for recitation in preparation for tests. The questions will become a self-test on the material. If you can answer the questions without looking at the notes, you have most likely learned the information. Record your questions here, along with the main ideas that you pull from the right-hand column.

How can you write recall-column questions? There are several ways to form questions for the recall column.

- Change the subheadings in textbooks or articles into questions.
- Use the questions at the end of the chapter if the author provides them.
- Write questions that use the words *why, when, where, how,* and *describe.*

Write main idea questions in the recall column. Usually there will be one question for each main idea. In order to create a question about a main idea and its details, you must understand the information. You need to think about the information in your notes. What is the idea being presented? Develop one question that pulls that information together. Refer to Chapter Four, page 49 if you have difficulty forming questions.

What is the summary? As in notes and mapping, write a summary at the end of your notes. Remember to write the summary in your words but include the main ideas in the order that they happen.

Look at the example below. See how all the parts of SSS are used. The topic is *killer smoke.* There are four main ideas: cause of death in fires, how to control smoke, cost of smoke control, and benefits of smoke control. Under each main idea you will find a number of details which help you remember the important points.

THE SUMMARY SHEET SYSTEM

RECALL	NOTES
	Killer Smoke (TOPIC)
Why does smoke kill more people than fire does?	**Causes (MAIN IDEA)** 80% die of smoke not fire e.g. MGM fire 1980 84 killed 12 by fire Smoke produces toxic clouds
How can smoke be controlled in a fire?	**Controlling Smoke (MAIN IDEA)** Vent smoke out by using air conditioners and blow out with fans Pressurized air Add system when constructing new buildings
Why is it reasonable to smoke-proof a building?	**Cost (MAIN IDEA)** Not high considering deaths Adds $1 per square foot to building cost Lowers insurance rates
What are the benefits of having smoke controlled facilities?	**Benefits (MAIN IDEA)** • Saves lives • Reduces lawsuits • Helps firefighters in a fire
	SUMMARY Smoke kills more people than actual fire. There are effective and fairly inexpensive ways to control smoke. Installing a smoke control system saves lives and property.

Remember . . .

SSS is equally effective for taking notes from lectures or textbooks. However, to really do its job, SSS must be used promptly. The recall column, for writing main-idea questions, is designed as a study help. Abbreviate and use your own words whenever possible. By taking accurate notes you freeze information so you can organize and make sense of it later.

Outlining

Should you use an outline format? Probably not. The three systems we've described are easier to use than the outline. There are many disadvantages to outlining. Since most teachers don't present information in time-order sequence, students usually become confused about whether to use letters or number and where to place information in the outline. Students end up missing the big picture because they are too concerned with the outline format itself.

Practice and Win

Practice the three methods we've described. The more you use them, the less you'll have to work at the job. You'll quickly develop your own shorthand to help. Just be sure you can read what you've written after the notes sit awhile.

You probably will find that ı notes are most useful for short assignments, such as a chapter of history you must read overnight. Use subheadings as topics, or, if it's short, the chapter heading could be the only topic you list. Keep your ı notes as you go along. Use mapping for bigger projects or to help in studying for that big test. Refer to your ı notes when drawing your map to help you remember those little details as well as the big ideas.

Draw a map to help organize your plan for that huge writing project when you've got a stack of big ideas from different books, from magazine articles, or even from interviews. Get the picture before you write.

Don't forget to draw a quick map as you begin that 50-point essay question — the one that counts for a full quarter of your test grade. You drew one when you studied for the test; the new map will help you recall all the important landmarks you included then.

Try the SSS system, too. It can help to really organize complex, long-range work. But it also is the system that requires the most constant attention. You might find it most useful later in your high school career, or even in college.

6

Making Time for Time

It's ten o'clock, maybe even ten-thirty. You're tired, and you haven't finished your homework. Sound familiar? Lots of kids have trouble managing their time. Maybe you didn't allow yourself enough study time. Or perhaps you spent too much time reading your English assignment, something that's not due for three more weeks. Or you just dawdled a little too much.

This chapter will help you avoid such time crunches.

Beating the Time Crunch

Scheduling your day or week does not mean planning every minute. It means making good use of your time. To get involved in managing your time, you must first analyze how you use your time. Ask yourself these questions:

How do I spend my time now?
Do I usually spend my time productively?
How much time do I waste?
Are there ways I could use my time better?

Be honest. There's no point in fudging. You already want to improve your study skills, otherwise you wouldn't be this far along in our book. You wouldn't be unusual if your answers reveal huge holes in your time-management scheme. In fact, you wouldn't want to get rid of all the holes — everybody needs a little just-goofing-off time. But even the most efficient person can still find ways to hone time-management skills even more sharply. Here are some strategies.

Lists, lists, lists. The first strategy is making a list of what you would like to accomplish for one day and then ranking what's on the list into three categories:

A — most important
B — next important
C — least important

Keep flexible. Certain situations may cause you to trade times or change the ordering of your list. If this happens, be sure to make a new list and rank the items. Now practice this idea with the following list.

Let's say you have eight things to do today. Rank order the tasks with the letters A, B, or C to show which you need to do first and which can wait.

_____ 1. doing my homework today

_____ 2. making a good effort in all my classes today

_____ 3. cleaning my room today

_____ 4. eating breakfast this morning

_____ 5. talking to my friends today

_____ 6. studying for the math test on Friday

_____ 7. working on my science project due next week

_____ 8. doing the chores I have at home

Now make your own list.

Daily Organization Chart

		Day	**10-22-92**

To-Do List	A B C	Estimated Completion Time	Date Completed and Actual Completion Time
Basketball practice	*A*	*2.0*	*2.5*
Math p. 56 #1 - 27 (odd only)	*A*	*.5*	*1.0*
Call for bowling lane- Fri. nite	*B*	*.1*	*.1*
Poetry Album- due 1/23	*B*	*1.0*	—
Wash gym uniform	*A*	*1.0*	—
Buy Mom's birthday present	*C*	*1.0*	—
			3.6

Do another one for the week. It might be useful to make a grid with the days of the week, like a row from the calendar.

Weekly List

Monday	Tuesday	Wednesday	Thursday	Friday	Weekend
24 *Spelling MP 7 59 - 66*	25 *Tab order form due Bring gram book*	26 *Math quiz Notetaking T: Witch M F: Prejudice*	27 *Science Fair Packets distributed Spelling Story*	28 *Mrs. Piccolo collecting notebooks -- Report Due*	*D a n c e*

Now that you've made a daily and weekly list, it's time to think about a monthly list, or perhaps even one that covers the whole grading period. A calendar format will really be useful for that so you can list all the events that are coming up. You'll want to schedule such things as the class trip to the amusement park, final exam dates, your best friend's birthday, school holidays, due dates for projects and papers — any event you need to keep track of.

Such dates are called *fixed commitments*. Most adults have to keep long-term calendars. People in business, industry, and government keep daily, weekly, and long-term calendars. They'd be lost without them, missing appointments and deadlines, or having to be in two places at once, an impossible task no matter how fast you are.

The example below will give you an idea of what a student's monthly list might look like.

Monthly Planner

Month	November

Monday	Tuesday	Wednesday	Thursday	Friday	Weekend
3 end 1st quarter	4 read last 2 ch Witch of Blackbird Pond	5 atmosphere report due	6 quiz- witch of Bl Pond Shawn's B-day	7 Library research Soc St report	
10 bring grammar book	11 Spelling MP 5 41-50	12 teacher recognition day Lincoln Center trip	13 ditto - - Witch of Bl. Pond due	14 grammar wk shts due Soc St Algebra test-unit 3	rough draft due Monday
17 grammar pp. 235-6 worksht Witch of Bl. Pond	18 Test Witch of Bl. pond	19 Spelling MP 6 51-58	20 Thanksgiving RECESS	21	Check: footnote bibliography format
24 Spelling MP 7 59-66	25 Tab order form due Bring Gram book	26 Math quiz Notetaking: T: witch MF : Prejudice	27 Science Fair packets distributed Spelling Story	28 Mrs. Piccolo collecting notebooks Report due	Dance
31 Basketball tryouts start		11-12 11-19 11-26	Take instrument		

What it'll take. The amount of homework due the next day as well as projects and papers due over the next few weeks will determine how much time you need to study each day. In order to plan, you'll have to figure out how long it will take you to complete each assignment. Look at the work and predict what it'll take to do the job. Such a prediction not only allows you to plan your time, it'll help you keep on track while you're doing the work. It's a lot easier to get the job done when you have a deadline to meet.

Look at the assignments due tomorrow. If you have ten math problems to complete, six pages from your earth science textbook to read and take notes about, and a two-minute speech for language arts, how much time will you need for study that night? Before starting, write down your estimate of how long it will take you to complete each task. Then do the work, checking after you finish, how close you were to your estimate. The more you do it, the better you will become at predicting the time it takes.

Break-up, shake-up. Larger assignments, such as that big language arts speech that will make up a large part of your grade in the class, can quickly turn into a muddle without a system. So how do you plan your work time for such a project? Try breaking the assignment into small chunks, estimating the amount of time needed to finish each chunk. For example:

Small chunk	Time needed
select the topic	10 min
gather information (at home, library, or school)	2 hrs
take notes from the information you gathered	4 hrs
arrange them in logical order	1 hr
write speech	1 hr
practice giving speech	1 hr
edit or revise speech	30 min
memorize speech	1 hr

The amount of time needed for each chunk will vary enormously from student to student. What's important is dividing the work into small parts and organizing how you will use your time to finish the assignment on schedule.

An hour, a year, a million years? Being able to accurately estimate the time a job will take is really impor-

tant. You don't want to have to choose between staying up until midnight to finish an English essay due the next day or simply not turning it in because it took an extra hour for you to get through a difficult math assignment earlier in the evening. Before you begin a study session, ask yourself these questions:

1. Do I know what the assignment is asking me to do?
2. How long do I estimate this assignment will take me to complete?
3. Do I have to break the task down into several manageable parts? If yes, how many?

After the study session, ask yourself these questions.

1. How long did it actually take me to complete the assignment?
2. Did I concentrate and stay on task?
3. Did I overestimate or underestimate the time I needed?
4. What can I do differently next time to improve my performance?

Homework

Homework is a part of school and learning. It's your opportunity to find out what you understand and what you still need to learn. It's the teacher's opportunity to find out what you can do on your own and to see how you're doing. To manage your homework better, first ask yourself the following questions.

What is the assignment?
Did I write the assignment in my notebook?
When is the assignment due?
Is the work easy or hard?
Do I understand the assignment?
Do I have enough information to do the assignment?
When will I do the assignment?
Where will I do the assignment?
How much time should this assignment take?

Should you do the easy work first or last? That's up to you. Try it both ways and see which you like best.

Should you work alone, or with others? We think it's good to work with others when possible. Start out with one study partner at first, and then gradually work your way into group study. Be careful whom you choose, though. Hard-working study partners will help you stay on task and practice your smart-learning skills.

Like goals, there are short- and long-term homework assignments. Short-term assignments are due the next class period. They usually give you a chance to practice the lesson you had that day. Long-term assignments may be due in a week, a month, or at the end of the semester.

They will require careful planning, including the strategies we outlined above — making lists, estimating and predicting time needed, and breaking work into chunks.

Homework time should be a part of your daily routine. Make time slots in your busy day in both the morning and the afternoon or evening. And don't be fooled by those days when you have no homework. Use them to work on long-term assignments.

Remember . . .

You're more likely to succeed in school if you manage your time. Smart learners keep track of important upcoming events and study at definite times. They develop daily, weekly, and monthly to-do lists.

If you set limits on the time you plan to study each time you begin an assignment, you should see two interesting outcomes: study time will gradually decrease and more information will be stored in long-term memory because of your higher level of concentration.

7

The Real Test

You've read the assignment, taken notes, and studied them. Now it's time for the test. How do you feel? Well prepared or scared to death? If you are one of the millions of people who suffer from test anxiety you may find this chapter very comforting.

Debunking the Myths

Now that you know you're not alone in your fear, it's time to "demythtify" the following beliefs.

MYTH 1

A little studying goes a long way. Over-studying will cause you to forget the material.

FACT 1

Information must be in your long-term memory before you have it available for the test. Your short-term memory cannot hold enough to get you through the entire test. The only way information gets into long-term memory is for you to rehearse it again and again.

MYTH 2

Studying silently and alone is the best way to prepare for a test.

FACT 2

Studying out loud with a friend, or in a study group is more effective because it allows you to put information into long-term memory through your eyes, ears, and mouth. This multi-sensory approach helps you rehearse the material. Often friends can supply information that you missed.

MYTH 3

Studying and rereading are the same thing.

FACT 3

Studying is more than reading. Active reading means that you have organized information with i notes, mapping, and SSS. Reading is not enough. You must review the information so that it makes sense and is stored in your long-term memory.

MYTH 4

Teachers never give enough information about the test beforehand.

FACT 4

Many students do not know how to ask teachers the right kinds of questions to get the information they want.

MYTH 5

All tests are alike.

FACT 5

Tests differ and preparation for each kind is different. True and false, multiple choice, and matching tests are all recognition tests. The answers for the questions are given to you. You have to recognize or identify the correct answer and mark it. Fill in the blanks, short answer, and essay tests all require you to supply the answer from memory. They demand much more practice and rehearsal during test preparation.

MYTH 6

Begin at the beginning of the test and work your way to the end.

FACT 6

Certain sections of a test may be worth more points than others. Those that are worth more should receive more of your time. Essay questions are usually worth more than multiple choice questions. Likewise, certain parts of the test may be easier and take less time than others. If you do them first, you will have more time for the difficult parts. Check the test carefully so you understand the value of each part of the test.

MYTH 7

Don't bother to check over the test when you finish. Work up to the last minute.

FACT 7

Hurrying to get everything done before time runs out causes careless errors. It is easy to leave out words, number an answer wrong, transpose numbers, or get mixed up on the answer sheets. Plan a few minutes at the end so that you have time to locate and fix problem areas. Always check that you have put your name on the paper as you hand it in.

MYTH 8

Cramming for a test is the most effective way to get good grades.

FACT 8

Cramming means putting lots of information into short-term memory in a short amount of time (usually the night before the test) with the hope that it will stay there during the test. That is not a physical possibility. Effective studying begins several days or even weeks in advance of the test — for short periods of time. Rehearsing the information puts it into long-term storage where you have access to it during the test. Cramming can actually make you forget the information. Your brain needs time to sort through the information and put it into clusters already in long-term memory. This process will be interrupted if you cram.

MYTH 9

Changing answers on a test is a bad practice.

FACT 9

Changing answers is neither bad nor good. Many times an answer to one question can be found in other questions. Take advantage of that help. Sometimes your memory supplies the answer very quickly. In that case, it is probably the correct answer.

MYTH 10

When in doubt, guess or flip a coin.

FACT 10

Guessing is reasonable if you have nothing to lose by guessing. Some tests have a penalty for guessing. That is done by counting the wrong answers twice and subtracting them from the correct answers. On a test with a guessing penalty, DO NOT GUESS. It is better to leave an answer blank.

Getting Ready

If you were planning to climb Mt. McKinley in Alaska, you wouldn't simply wake up one day, roll out of bed and into your clothes, jump onto a jet to Fairbanks, hop on a smaller plane and fly to the base of the mountain, then just get out and start walking.

If you want to get to the top, you'd prepare for months. You'd train in mountain-climbing skills, you'd do physical conditioning, you'd outfit yourself with the proper equipment. You'd really plan.

Like the mountain, a test can loom awfully large in your life. But often, students fail to recognize the need for preparation. They simply hop out of bed, jump into their clothes, and go to class, where Mt. McKinley looms, waiting on their desks in the form of a test that they haven't really prepared for.

It doesn't usually take months of physical fitness training to take a test successfully (although adequate eating and a good night's sleep are important). And it doesn't take special climbing boots and foul weather gear, tents and oxygen bottles.

But it does take some tools, ones you should now have in your smart learning tool kit, and careful planning. To get ready for a test, here's what you need.

Survival supplies. Your textbook, your í notes, your maps, and SSS are your sources of information. Your notebook contains everything you will need if you have used it as we have suggested in this book.

Time and space. You need time to collect your thoughts, see the connections among the facts, vocabulary, and ideas presented in the information, and determine how all the pieces fit together. Your brain needs time to cluster (gather, organize, and make sense of) information. That's why cramming is inefficient. Your study space must be uncluttered and neat. You need room to spread out all the materials you've created.

Know the opposition. This is supplied by the teacher who tells you what kind of test you will have (true and false, matching, multiple choice, short answer, essay); how many questions; and how much time is allotted for taking the test. The teacher expects you to know how to study for each kind of test, how to answer the questions, and what materials you will need to take the test.

Listen to your teacher. Teachers use verbal cues, such as repeating important points or emphasizing ideas by saying them louder, to give hints about what is really important. Sometimes they have pet phrases such as:

A word to the wise . . .
You can expect to see this material again . . .
A smart student will learn this for later . . .
Success in this class depends on . . .
You'll get good grades in here if you . . .
There are two things to always remember about . . .
Now let me say that again . . .
Make sure you get this down . . .
I think it is really important that you . . .

These clues should act as red flashing lights that signal important information is on the way. If you sit passively, only half listening, you will miss out. And missing out on information will effect your grade.

Tipping the balance. The following list will remind you of important tips before, during, and after the test. You just may want to memorize this list.

- *Overlearn the material.* There is no such thing as studying too much for a test. Overlearning the material will reduce your text anxiety. Overlearning is not cramming.
- *Be on time for the test.* Coming too early and listening to other students worry about the test, or arriving late will increase your nervousness.
- *Write your name on the paper the minute you get the test.*
- *Make a map* of what you know to help you remember specific information before you attempt to answer essay questions.
- *Read, don't skim, the directions.* They may be different for each part of the test. If possible, circle key words in the directions so you complete each section correctly.
- *Manage your time carefully during the test.* Determine which sections are worth the most points. Take the time to answer these questions well. You might need to do the multiple choice and true and false first so you will have plenty of time left to write the essay answers. Answer essay questions completely and neatly.
- *Check over your answers before handing in your test.* Errors result in lower grades.
- *Ask to see your corrected test.* Analyze the errors you made. You will become test-wise.

Remember . . .

Prepare for tests in an organized way. You will improve your performance and be less nervous. Keep a positive attitude, study ahead, and find out the kind of test for which you are preparing. Take notes (î, mapping, and SSS). Study for short periods over several days. Avoid cramming. When you get the test, write your name on it. For each section of the test, read the directions carefully and check the point values of each item. Decide whether you should do the items with the most points first. Memorize the test-taking tips. Before you hand in the test make sure your name is on the paper and that your answers are neat and orderly.

8

Going for the Gold

Goal-setting and decision-making go hand in hand. In this chapter you'll learn how to set long- and short-term goals as well as how to use a decision-making strategy. When you set goals and learn how to make good decisions, you'll not only manage your studies better, but your whole life, now, and in the future.

Why Set Goals?

"If you don't know where you are going, any road will take you there." So goes the old saying. Instead of gambling with your life, we hope you will have some dreams — some strong ideas of where you want to go. Learning to set goals will help you realize your dreams. Having goals inspires action.

Goals give you direction in life and provide the necessary road map for success. Goals, plans, and actions stem from problems. Problems call for action. Goals are things you want to accomplish. Plans are the general strategies for achieving goals. In working toward accomplishing the goals you set for yourself, consider the following questions. Are your goals:

- specific in nature? . . . What do you want?
- measurable? . . . How do you know when you get it?
- specific in duration? . . . How long will it take?
- attainable? . . . Are you kidding yourself?
- compatible? . . . Is it worth it?
- motivational? . . . Why bother?

Completing goals requires planning, making clear decisions, and a willingness to devote your talents and energy in working toward that goal. The more you set goals and achieve them, the more self-confident and motivated you become.

There are five steps in setting a goal:

1. *Put the goal into words.* Writing freezes ideas and keeps them from disappearing.

2. *Develop a personal plan of action.* When you plan ahead you give yourself lots of time to think the plan through.

3. *Plan to overcome the traps that prevent you from reaching your goal.* Predicting what might happen helps you avoid problems. So does figuring out solutions for potential problems.

4. *List emotional factors that will occur along the way.* Don't let others interfere with your goals. Sometimes people say things that might influence you to give up. You need to fight those feelings. Make plans to deal with situations before they happen.

5. *Nurture your desire and determination.* They will keep you on track and help you reach your goal.

Right now and the next day. Short-term goals need to be realistic and reachable in a short period of time. These goals give you immediate feedback on whether or not you were successful in your effort. Writing short-term goals for yourself is a good way to begin writing and establishing long-term goals.

Here are some examples of short-term goals — the sort of things you'll have to do daily to be successful.

Get at least a B grade on my science test Friday.

Complete all my homework before the Monday night football game.

Listen and take notes in my science class today.

Ask questions of my math teacher about the material I don't understand.

Get to every class early this week so I can review my notes before class starts.

The big picture. Long-term goals require a great deal of planning and more time to complete than short-term goals, but they are definitely something you want to learn how to do. At first you will most likely work on short-term goals. But as the year goes on and you are getting ready for high school, you will need to begin thinking of setting some long-term goals for your high school years. When you're in high school, you'll need to develop long-term goals for college and your career.

Here are some examples of long-term goals. Notice that these are the kind of things you must do over time. Long-term goals help you check where you've been, whether you're on the right track, and what you will do next.

My Goals

_____ go to Ohio State University after high school

_____ collect a complete set of 1991 Topps baseball cards

_____ get three A's on my first report card

_____ be a teacher

_____ attend a college preparatory high school

_____ own a car by age 20

_____ take a drama workshop next summer

_____ be on the honor roll at least twice this school year

After you set your goals: it's important to plan how you will reach them. And don't forget to build in some rewards for when you reach your goals!

Below are two examples that show how goals were planned.

Short-term goal: to finish my homework before the Monday night football game. To reach my goal I plan to:

— do as much as possible during the study period in each class

— go straight home from school

— turn off the radio or TV, have a snack, and then start working on my homework

— work on math first, then English, science, and history

— work until I have all of my homework done — working in 30-minute segments, taking a 10-minute break between each

— reward myself when I reach my goal by watching the football game

Long-term goal: to buy a good stereo sound-system unit a year from now. The approximate cost will be $600, which I will earn myself. To reach my goal I plan to:

1. mow lawns this summer and save 50% of my earnings
2. charge $10 per lawn
3. do two lawns per day three days per week
4. work from June 1 until September 7
5. $10 per lawn × 2 lawns × 3 days × 15 weeks means I will make $900
6. save the rest of the money during the year (From the $10 per week my parents give me, I will save $5 per week. I will save a total of $630.)
7. find out if the unit is on sale and which store has the best buy
8. buy the unit in September
9. treat myself by listening to my music without disturbing others

A yellow caution light. Sometimes you may not be able to reach your goal because you miscalculated the five steps in goal setting. Or you didn't have enough information. Or you were faced with circumstances over which you had no control. It would be difficult to keep on track if there were a major earthquake in your town, for example, or a huge flood, or even a revolution. But often, the obstacle is a more everyday problem, such as procrastination, fear of failure, peer pressure, poor attitude, not eating right, or not getting enough sleep. You get the idea. Such obstacles are called traps, and any one of them can prevent you from reaching your goals. You must work to avoid traps, and learning how to deal with them is a sign of maturity.

On the other hand, there are situations that may cause you to change or revise your goals. There really might be an earthquake that disrupts school for weeks. Or you might get sick during the semester and miss four weeks of classes. When you return to school, you may find that you don't have time to reach your goal of making at least four B's this grading period. So you may decide to change your goal to making two B's and two C's. This would be realistic given the circumstances.

Making reasonable changes is something everyone has to do from time to time. Setting realistic goals allows you to take charge of your life and to make things go your way. Look for chances to set goals and work towards them.

Making Up Your Mind

You make hundreds of decisions each day. Big ones, small ones, important ones, and lots of not-so-important ones. Smart decision making, like smart learning, will put you more in control of your life and will help make it good.

Most of your decisions will be minor ones, such as when you should study for a test, and whether or not to go to the Friday night dance. You probably will be able to make these small decisions without much thought — just a quick consideration of the arguments and a decision.

Some decisions are more complex and have a greater impact on your life. For example, you may have to decide which course of study you want to pursue in high school in order to get ready for the career you have in mind. Or you might have to decide whether or not to hang around certain kids because of the kinds of activities they're involved in. If you act too quickly or impulsively, you may regret your decisions later.

When you make decisions, there are *intended outcomes*, those things that you know will have an influence on how your decisions turns out. The following scenario is an example of an intended outcome.

> You have decided that there is a problem between you and your parents. They are upset that you always need to be told to do your chores, that your room is messy, and that you don't seem to take things seriously. To make things better you decide to organize your time better so you will have more time each day for chores and studying. Your long-term goal is to make the honor roll. You can anticipate that if you do what you say, things will improve greatly between your parents and you.

But there may also be unintended outcomes that you did not consider.

> You forgot to consider your friends. Now that you have less time, they are upset with you because you are not hanging around them as much. As your grades improve, they begin to rag you about your success and accuse you of being a different person. They begin to ignore you.

Some decisions you make will be good ones. You can feel that they were correct and you can measure what happened against what you expected to happen. Some decisions are mistakes. No matter how carefully you study a problem, you may make a choice that you will be unhappy with later. When you know you made a bad decision — that's the time to correct it. Stubbornness and pride must be put aside. Keep your losses to a minimum. Everyone makes mistakes. Bad decisions sometimes come with punishments attached. Take your punishment and don't make excuses. You will benefit a great deal from your mistakes.

Poor decisions come from acting emotionally, impulsively, or not acting at all. Not making a decision is making a decision. It is called procrastination. This is the worst kind of decision making because you are leaving what will happen to you in the hands of others who don't know how you feel, what you want, or don't care about your feelings. You are giving up control of your life.

A word to the wise. There is no one method for making decisions. But if you follow a rational system, such as the one we describe below, you improve your chances of making the right decision. Our system, PRoblem-Alternatives-Consequences-Take-Action-Success, PRAC-TAS for short, has five basic steps.

P > identify your *PRoblem*

R

A – list all the *Alternatives* or options you can think of

C – determine the good and bad *Consequences* of each alternative

T > *Take Action* on one of the alternatives

A

S – evaluate your plan to determine the amount of *Success*

Look at the following example to see how you can use PRACTAS to make decisions.

The final chapter test in social studies is scheduled for next Friday. If you get a 90% or higher on this test you will raise your grade average to a B. You need an 80% to keep a C. If you score below 70% you will get a D.

PR Do I want to get a B, C, or D in this course?

A	C	TA
What are my alternatives?	What are the consequences?	Which do I follow?
1. Study for the 90%	Plan to study one hour each night. Say no to other activities. I will feel ready for the test. I will receive a B for the course and make the honor roll. My parents will be happy.	
2. Study just enough to get an 80%.	Plan to study the night before the test I might not be ready and could get a D I receive a C for the course My parents might be unhappy.	
3. Not to study at all	I receive a D for the course. A D would prevent me from doing school activities next year.	

S How successful was my decision?

Which would you follow? Why?

⚡Remember . . .

Setting short-term and long-term goals is one way to take the chance out of your life. Using a system like PRAC-TAS will help you make smart decisions.

You did well to work your way through this book. It shows you have the strength of character to become a successful person. Congratulations! Now comes the real challenge — using the techniques in this book daily. If you return to this book again and again "Smart Learning" will become second nature to you. Almost without thinking, you will apply the PREP system, the î notemaking technique, and the PRACTAS strategy for making decisions. In these ways you will learn more, learn faster, and get better grades all around.

You are on your way!

Index

Do you want to get your act together?

The Skillful Learner™ **STUDENT ORGANIZER** developed by William Christen and Thomas Murphy makes it easy to get it together and to follow the techniques in *Smart Learning*.

The Skillful Learner™ **STUDENT ORGANIZER** includes:

- ➤ Durable poly binder
- ➤ Erasable Monthly Planners
- ➤ Erasable Daily Planners
- ➤ Erasable To Do List
- ➤ Accessory Vinyl Pouch
- ➤ Erasable Pen
- ➤ Special Eraser
- ➤ Notemaking System Paper
- ➤ Eight Index Tabs (printed with important things to remember about the study and learning techniques in *Smart Learning)*

You can use this one binder for all your subjects. You'll never be more organized and together than with **The Skillful Organizer**™ **STUDENT ORGANIZER.**

Price: $29.95, plus $4.00 shipping and handling.

ORDER FORM

To order fill out the form below and send check or money order to:

Grayson Bernard Publishers
223 S. Pete Ellis Drive, Suite 12B
Bloomington, IN 47408

Please send me _____ copies of **The Skillful Learner**™ **STUDENT ORGANIZER.** I have enclosed $29.95 plus $4.00 shipping and handling for each.

Name_____

Address_____

City _____ State _____ Zip _____

Books for Home and School
from Grayson Bernard Publishers

➤ *Smart Learning: A Study Skills Guide for Teens*
by William Christen and Thomas Murphy

Learn to focus study time and energy for fantastic
results the whole family will be proud of!

➤ *Intermediate Grammar: A Student's Resource Book*
by Carl B. Smith, Ph.D.

A student's grammatical lifesaver! Includes
separate grammar and punctuation handbook for
quick, easy reference.

➤ *Elementary Grammar: A Child's Resource Book*
by Carl B. Smith, Ph.D.

A handy source of answers and explanations for
young learners and their parents.

➤ *The Confident Learner: Help Your Child Succeed in School*
by Marjorie R. Simic, Melinda McClain, and Michael Shermis

A guide to everything from homework to high
motivation—a confidence builder for both parents
and children!

➤ *Help Your Child Read and Succeed: A Parents' Guide*
by Carl B. Smith, Ph.D.

Practical, caring advice with skill-building activities for
parents and children from a leading expert in the field.

➤ *Expand Your Child's Vocabulary: A Twelve-Week Plan*
by Carl B. Smith, Ph.D.

A dozen super strategies for vocabulary growth.

*Find these valuable resources at your favorite bookstore, or use
the order form on the next page to have these books sent directly
to you.*

❦

Order Information

☎ To order by phone, call toll-free 1-800-356-9315 and use your VISA, MasterCard, or American Express.

✉ To order books by mail, fill out the form below and send check or money order to:

Grayson Bernard Publishers
P. O. Box 5247, Dept. B
Bloomington, IN 47407

Qty.	Title	Author	Unit Cost	Total
	Smart Learning	Christen/ Murphy	$10.95	
	Intermediate Grammar	Smith, C.	$16.95	
	Elementary Grammar	Smith, C.	$13.95	
	The Confident Learner	Simic, M.	$ 9.95	
	Help Your Child Read and Succeed	Smith, C.	$12.95	
	Expand Your Child's Vocabulary	Smith, C.	$ 7.95	

Shipping & Handling:

☐ Book Rate: $2.00 for the first book plus
   $1.00 for each additional book.

☐ Air Mail: $3.00 for the first book plus
   $1.50 for each additional book.

Subtotal	
Shipping & Handling	
IN residents add 5% sales tax	
TOTAL	

Send books to:

Name _____

Address _____

City_____State _____ Zip _____

Prices subject to change.

Your satisfaction is guaranteed.
Any book may be returned within 60 days for a full refund.

A Success Story!

In praise of **The Skillful Learner**™ Program:

> " We have been using the learning and study skills techniques of Christen and Murphy for five years with all of our middle level students. In that time we have seen remarkable, positive changes in our students. Students on the A and B honor roll have increased to 55-60% of the student body. We have even received commendations from parents because they see their children making extra efforts on academic pursuits at home. "

—Jack Welton, Director of Middle Childhood Education, Putnam County Schools, West Virginia

You can create a success story too, with the help of *Smart Learning* and **The Skillful Learner**™ **STUDENT ORGANIZER**.

To order either one of these fine products, see the order information on the previous pages or call (812) 331-8182.

GRAYSON BERNARD
PUBLISHERS